M000230141

Baby Proofing Basics

by Vicki Lansky

Book Peddlers
Minnetonka, MN

SPECIAL EDITORIAL THANKS TO:
> Kathryn Ring
> Julie Surma
> Rose Ann Soloway, National Capitol Poison Center
> Ann Pavlin, Office of Information-CPSC
> Stephanie Tombrello, SafetyBeltSafe USA
> Jeffrey Michael, US Dept of Transportation
> Cheryl Kim
> *and to*

Michael Lerner & Michael Bernstein of SAFETY FIRST
whose vision was responsible for this book.

Other titles by Vicki Lansky include:

Feed Me I'M Yours	*Kids Cooking*
Taming of the CANDY Monster	*Dear Babysitter Handbook*
Practical Parenting Tips/Yrs 1-5	*KoKo Bear's Big Earache*
Toilet Training	*KoKo Bear's New Potty*
Welcoming Your 2nd Baby	*New Baby at KoKo Bear's*
Birthday Parties	*Divorce Book for Parents*
101 Ways Tell Child I Love You	*Another Use For...*

Book Design: The Book Peddlers
Book Cover and Illustrations: Steve Boris

ISBN NUMBER   0-916773-28-0

First printing, February 1991
All rights reserved
Copyright © 1991 SAFETY FIRST

This book may not be reproduced in whole or part without the
permission of Safety First, For information, contact:
Safety First, Chestnut Hill, MA 02167 (617) 964-7744

Published simultaneouosly for the book trade by
BOOK PEDDLERS, MINNETONKA, MN 55345, 612/912-0036
and distributed by Publishers Group West, Emeryville, CA

12 11 10 9 8 7 6 5 4

Table of Contents

Introduction

In the beginning, God created this wonderful little, seemingly helpless baby who is basically immobile and reacts only to the stimuli of his or her environment. From your baby's beginning days, you will quickly be thrust into the role of your child's protector. The world now becomes a source of learning as well as danger. And, now—forever—you will either act or feel like protecting your child. And beginning from the time your child can turn over, your role will be very specific.

Birth to 4 months: While seeming limited in mobility, babies can squirm, wiggle and even turn over, getting themselves into dangerous situations. Don't leave even the youngest baby unattended on a high surface and check all corners he or she may be able to scoot into.

4 months to 7 months: Babies begin to roll over, creep backward or even forward, sit up, and put every possible object into their mouths. They're also very interested in everything. Watch the environment!

7 months to 1 year: Crawling, standing, walking and climbing developments make toddlers a moving menace to themselves. There is the danger of falls and pulling heavy objects down on themselves. Anything may be ingested so accidental poisoning becomes a real threat. Childproof thoroughly, then always be on the alert!

Up to 5 years: Running (and falling), curiosity with water, the ability to dismantle most anything, and lack for fear makes children a real danger to themselves. Active children, without the understanding of the consequences of their actions, will continue to need to be monitored and watched, despite their apparent understanding of your words and warnings.

What we know to be true is that most accidents are preventable. We know, unfortunately through the tragedies of other families where and what causes so many of these accidents. We must learn from the experiences of others so we CAN protect our children. That's what we've tried to share with you on the following pages. What you buy, where you put it, and how you use it are important lessons to learn. This knowledge, coupled with responsible surveillance of your children, will provide you with your best protection for the health and well-being of your family.

Fortunately we are not totally left to personal vigilance alone in the product area. The Federal government has come to our aid through the efforts of the Consumer Product Safety Commission (CPSC). The Consumer Product Safety Commission is an independent regulatory commission whose mandate it is to protect the consumer from "unreasonable risk of injury" from products. If you have questions about recall information or want to report a product injury, call 800-638-2772 or write CPSC at 5401 Westbard

Avenue, Bethesda, MD 20816.

The Juvenile Products Manufacturers Association, Inc. (JPMA) is a trade association with over 250 member companies in the US and Canada that manufacture and/or distribute infant products. The association has always been conscious about helping consumers keep babies safe.

In order to achieve this, JPMA initiated an extensive Safety Certification program in 1976. An independent group, the American Society for Testing and Materials (ASTM), was asked by JPMA to develop safety standards for high chairs. ASTM is a highly respected non-profit organization that develops standards for materials and products in many industries. To date, hundreds of models of high chairs, play yards, carriages, strollers, walkers and expandable gates and enclosures are JPMA certified products. Manufacturers seeking the JPMA Safety Certification Seal submit their products voluntarily. Only those meeting the tough standards established by ASTM are awarded the JPMA seal.

Do be aware that not all problems with products are the fault of manufacturers. Many mishaps and accidents occur because parents have not assembled a product correctly, have not read directions carefully, are using the product in the wrong ways, are not properly supervising its use or are unaware of its potential hazards. Unfortunately,

EVEN SAFE PRODUCTS CAN BECOME
UNSAFE IF THEY ARE MISUSED OR
USED INCORRECTLY.

Vicki Lansky

♥ 1 ♥

Baby Proofing Room by Room

Accidents, not illnesses, cause most child deaths—some 400 children under four years old die of accidents every month in the United States. The major causes of death or injury to children under 14 are car accidents, drownings, burns, falls and choking/poisoning.

Two major elements are involved in keeping your child safe from harm in your home. First, careful, thoughtful childproofing of every room in the house. And second, your constant, loving vigilance. Never underestimate the powers of a child. "I didn't think she could do that," is the tragic cry of many parents of bright, curious children who were only investigating their environments.

The best way to find the dangers that can cause harm to your child is to look at your house from the child's vantage point. Get down on your hands and knees and examine everything carefully and check for potential hazards. You'll find a world of fascinating things to pull on, squeeze, throw, crawl into and under, chew and swallow. You'll see sharp edges and corners that can cut, objects that can break and turn into weapons of destruction, furniture that can be climbed on.

Your object as a parent is to make your house safe for your baby to explore. You want to eliminate dangers without being over-protective or inhibiting your child. No parent can prevent all accidents. As long as you prevent the serious ones—the fatal ones —you'll have done your job.

THE TIME TO CHILDPROOF YOUR HOUSE
IS BEFORE YOUR CHILD NEEDS IT,
OTHERWISE IT MIGHT BE TOO LATE!

BABY PROOFING THE KITCHEN

There are many potential possibilities for disaster in a kitchen. A few examples are: hot liquids and hot dishes, equipment that can cause burns, spills that make floors slippery leading to bad falls, cleaning chemicals that can poison, appliances that threaten electrocution, and sharp and heavy objects that can cause injury. There are many times when the best kitchen childproofing consists of a gate at the door, to keep your child out of the room altogether. And if that is not feasible, then be sure to:

> NEVER LEAVE A SMALL CHILD
> ALONE IN THE KITCHEN.

A collection of tips on kitchen safety is available from the Consumer Product Safety Commission. Send a postcard to Kitchens, Washington, DC 20207.

Appliances and Equipment

♥ Turn the handles of pots and pans in toward the back of the stove top so your child can't grab them and pull down hot food. Fry or boil foods on the back burners whenever possible.

♥ Don't allow a baby to play on the floor by the stove when you're cooking or you're setting the stage for disaster.

♥ Buy a stove guard so your child can't reach or touch the stove burners. Or look for a padded hanging "apron" for ovens with a pull down handle.

♥ Make controls on the front of a stove impossible for a baby to use. Remove and store them where only you can reach them when needed. Or it might be more convenient to buy stove knob covers. Stove knob covers may even fit your oven controls as well.

♥ Don't leave a boiling pot or a sizzling skillet unattended on the stove. Thousands of children suffer burns from hot liquids every year, mostly from kitchen accidents.

♥ Turn on the oven light when the oven's in use, if the door is glass, and teach your child that "light on" means "hands off." Be sure to leave the light on until the oven has cooled.

♥ Put out small stove top fires by covering flames with a pan cover or an inverted pot which will act as a lid. Or throw baking soda on the flames. NEVER POUR WATER ON A GREASE FIRE. It will cause the grease to splatter and burn you.

♥ Don't heat baby bottles in the microwave oven. The liquid heats unevenly, and while the part you test may be fine, another portion may be scalding. Because of steam buildup, glass and some plastic bottles can explode when taken from the oven.

♥ Get an appliance latch or safety strap that will make it impossible for your child to open conventional and microwave ovens, the dishwasher, the trash compactor, and the refrigerator. If you're buying new appliances, look into those that are equipped with safety locks.

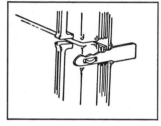 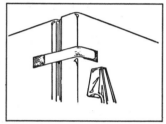

APPLIANCE LATCH   VELCRO APPLIANCE LATCH

♥ <u>Always</u> keep the dishwasher closed when you're not actually using it. (You can count on your baby being hurt on a sharp corner the one time it's left down!) Add detergent only when you're ready to run the machine, so your child won't have a chance to taste it. It's harmful if eaten.

♥ Whether your laundry appliances are in the kitchen or in a separate room, don't let your child play in or on them.

♥ Never leave an ironing board set up or folded up where a child might be able to pull it over.

Counter Tops, Cupboards and Tables

♥ Keep work surfaces as clear as possible so you can spot sharp or dangerous objects easily.

♥ Don't sit your baby on a counter where he or she can reach hot or dangerous items. When the baby's in the highchair, keep hot foods near the center of a table or at the back of a counter where they can't be reached.

♥ Keep appliance cords short by using cord shorteners which either wrap or wind up. Be especially careful of cords around toasters and other appliances that heat; they can be damaged by excess heat.

♥ Get in the habit of unplugging all counter top appliances after <u>every</u> use, in case your child manages to reach an "on" switch before you reach him or her. Put outlet covers on unused counter electrical sockets as an added precaution.

♥ Get cabinet and drawer guard latches to keep certain reachable cupboard doors and drawers off-limits to your baby. This may mean most of your cupboards. Remember that even such harmless-seeming items as toothpicks or bottle covers pose choking and other hazards to a baby or small child.

♥ Look into the various kinds of latches available to find the ones most appropriate for your kitchen and best suited to your needs. One kind, for example, must be installed with screws. Some plastic latches allow an adult to open a drawer wide enough to slip fingers in and release the safety hook from the latch by pressing down on it with one finger. Other latches slide through handles and the pressure needed to keep them closed can be managed by an adult but not by a child

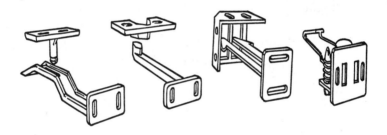

VARIOUS TYPES OF DRAWER AND CABINET LOCKS

♥ Do store safe-to-play-with pots and pans or plastic containers in one lower cupboard and let it be available for play, but be sure it's as far as possible from the stove and the busiest area of the kitchen.

General Kitchen Safety Rules

♥ Keep the kitchen trash container, with its hazard-ous sharp, pointed and otherwise dangerous con-tents, locked up in a broom closet or under the sink. Consider buying a self-locking garbage can or a

trash compactor, which, as long as you keep it
closed, keeps trash completely out of reach.

♥ Likewise, keep all cleaning materials, pesticides
and other dangerous substances locked up.

♥ Avoid pinched fingers by removing a swinging door
between kitchen and dining room or securing it in
an open position with a hook-and-eye latch or a
doorstop your child can't remove.

♥ Never leave an even partially full bucket, especially
in the five-gallon size, on the floor where a curious
child might fall into it head first and drown. Don't
feel that this advice is over-precautionary. There
are documented cases of such drownings.

♥ Use unbreakable dishes and glasses for feeding a
young child.

♥ Keep pet bowls and dishes out of a child's reach. A
cat's dish might be kept on a small table or counter
that's not used for food preparation and a dog's food
and water might be put in his outdoor fenced-in
area or in the basement or garage.

♥ Keep your playpen, if you use one in the kitchen, at
least two feet away from worktops and the stove.

♥ Put your stepstool away when it's not in use. It can
give a toddler a boost to the dangers of stove top or
counters.

♥ Clean up spills on the floor immediately so neither you nor your child will slip and fall. And don't use a wax that makes your floor slippery.

♥ Don't <u>ever</u> hold your baby in your arms while you cook; the possibilities for disaster are multiple. In the same vein, never try to carry your baby and a cup of coffee or other hot liquid at the same time.

Kitchen Storage

Store all cleaning materials and other dangerous substances in their original containers and <u>never</u> in familiar food containers such as milk or juice cartons, even though you are sure they are securely locked away where your child cannot get at them. (See page 138 for information on poisoning.)

Keep plastic wrap, and all sizes of plastic bags out of your child's reach, especially garbage and dry cleaning bags. (This warning obviously includes those in bedrooms, closets and the garage, as well as in the kitchen.) When you dispose of these items, tie them in knots so they cannot possibly be wrapped around a child's face or inhaled and cause suffocation. From 1980 to 1987, 112 children died when plastic bags covered their faces. Eighty percent of them were under a year old.

♥ Remember to keep boxes of kitchen wraps out of your child's reach. Their serrated cutting edges are as dangerous as your knives.

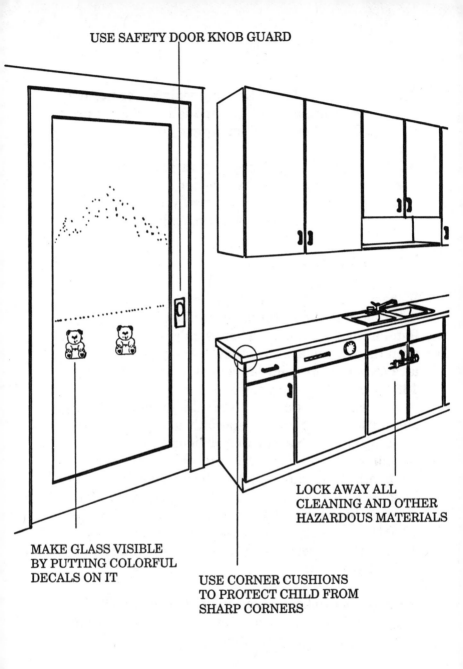

USE SAFETY DOOR KNOB GUARD

MAKE GLASS VISIBLE
BY PUTTING COLORFUL
DECALS ON IT

USE CORNER CUSHIONS
TO PROTECT CHILD FROM
SHARP CORNERS

LOCK AWAY ALL
CLEANING AND OTHER
HAZARDOUS MATERIALS

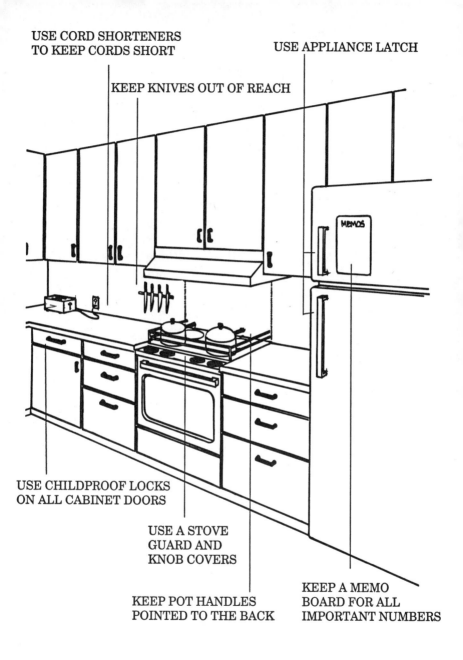

USE CORD SHORTENERS
TO KEEP CORDS SHORT

USE APPLIANCE LATCH

KEEP KNIVES OUT OF REACH

MEMOS

USE CHILDPROOF LOCKS
ON ALL CABINET DOORS

USE A STOVE
GUARD AND
KNOB COVERS

KEEP POT HANDLES
POINTED TO THE BACK

KEEP A MEMO
BOARD FOR ALL
IMPORTANT NUMBERS

♥ Keep all potentially dangerous kitchen utensils in securely latched drawers. Don't forget to include such items as apple corers, egg beaters, vegetable peelers and grapefruit spoons.

♥ Don't store crackers, cookies or other goodies above the stove, tempting your child to attempt the climb to reach them.

♥ Install a hook on the wall to hold long phone cords that a child could trip on or try to play with or get caught around the neck.

The Highchair

One of the most necessary pieces of baby equipment is also one of the most potentially dangerous. The Consumer Product Safety Commission estimates that in one year over 7,000 children were treated in hospital emergency rooms as a result of accidents involving highchairs.

Check the highchair you buy (or borrow) carefully to be sure it has a wide base and a tray that locks securely. Waist and crotch straps should not be attached to the tray. The buckle on the restraining strap should be easy to fasten. Caps and plugs on tubing on a metal chair should be firmly attached.

♥ Be sure the tray is locked after you put your baby into the highchair and <u>always</u> hook up the restraint system. It's important to keep the highchair clean, stuck-on food can interfere with the locking mechanics and cause deterioration of the restraint system.

♥ Watch your baby's fingers as you slide the tray on. When your child is old enough to understand, you might use the watchwords "Hands Up" to help make sure fingers are out of harm's way.

♥ Put bathtub decals or a rubber sink mat on a slippery highchair seat so your child is not prone to slipping down the seat.

♥ Be sure any item attaching a bottle or small toy to the highchair is no longer than 12 inches. Pacifiers can be attached to clothing with pacifier holders can be purchased in baby departments The ribbon on these should be no longer than 7". Longer string is a strangulation hazard.

♥ Never leave a baby alone in a room in the highchair, even with the safety strap securely fastened. (And remember, the highchair TRAY is <u>not</u> an adequate child-restraint!)

♥ Keep the highchair at a safe distance from the table or counters—any child can tip it over by pushing off with hands or feet. Standing up in the chair or rocking it back and forth can also cause it to tip.

♥ And teach older children not to climb on the highchair with or without a baby in it. That's equally dangerous.

HIGHCHAIRS MADE ACCORDING TO JPMA STANDARDS MUST HAVE:

• A strong frame, joints and seat that will withstand rough treatment.
• A strong restraining device to keep baby secured to the chair seat.
• A tray that stays in position once it is properly locked.
• An easy-to-clean finish that won't peel or bubble.
• Good balance and stability.
• Holes or openings designed not to catch fingers, toes or buttons.

BABY PROOFING THE BATHROOM

The bathroom is as full of dangers for your baby as the kitchen. The combination of water, attractive poisonous substances and intriguing appliances is fascinating to a curious child looking for entertainment.

The Bathroom "Furnishings"

♥ Keep the toilet lid down, or better yet, get a guard that actually locks it. It's important to prevent it from becoming a place for water play (and a dangerous opportunity for drowning). Children are often fascinated by the action of the swirling water.

HINGE MOUNTED LID LOCK

BOWL MOUNTED LID LOCK

♥ Get a soft spout cover for the bathtub. It will not only save your baby from bumps and bruises but will also help to avoid the possibility of hot water burns from a very hot spout. As an extra safety measure, face your child away from the faucet as you bathe him or her.

♥ Place soft inflated tub knob covers over cold and hot handles to prevent children from turning on tub water, especially the hot water which might scald them.

♥ Test the bath water on the inside of your wrist before putting your baby into the tub. Better yet, invest in a bath thermometer. When you've filled the tub, turn off the hot water before the cold, so the latter will flow through the faucet if your child manages to touch it.

♥ Keep the water temperature for your house set at about 120°—hot enough to clean clothes and dishes, yet not scalding. If you have no control over the water heater, check your hardware store for anti-scald aerators. Or retrofit a valve with a special temperature-sensitive spring called an actuator to stop the flow of scalding water.

♥ Put non-skid appliques on the bottom of the tub to prevent slips, or use a rubber mat.

♥ Never leave water in the tub when it's not in use. A toddler can fall in and drown in as little as two to three inches of water.

♥ Consider using a three-legged bathtub ring seat to help keep your child secure during a bath. You might also think about using a shampoo visor if a fearful child fights hair washing vigorously.

♥ **Do not, under any circumstances, leave a child under five years old unattended in the tub.** If you can't stand to let a phone ring, unplug it or use an answering machine. If you must leave the room for any reason, wrap your child in a towel and take him or her with you.

Medicines and Prescriptions

Medicines are usually best kept under lock and key and/or in a room other than the bathroom, such as the kitchen, despite the inconvenience. Be aware that the stepstool that makes it possible for your toddler to reach the bathroom sink will also help him to reach the medicine cabinet or other high and interesting places in the bathroom. Remember, HIGH IS NOT NECESSARILY SAFE. But at the very least, keep items out of sight as well as out of reach.

♥ Get a special locking medicine chest (or improvise—
even a tackle box may work for you) or use a
childproof lock on your existing cabinet. Open it
only to get something out and lock it again before
you leave the room.

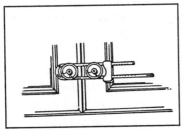

CABINET SLIDE LOCK   MEDICINE CABINET LOCK

♥ Be sure all medicines are in child-resistant containers (and that they're kept tightly closed).

♥ Don't save old prescription medicines, and above all,
don't <u>use</u> them for your children. Flush them down
the toilet. Illnesses that may seem identical don't
always require the same treatment and outdated
prescriptions can do more harm than good.

♥ And don't save prescription containers—when the
medicine is gone or outdated, dispose of the bottle
or box.

♥ Overdosing on children's vitamins rates among the
top phone calls received by Poison Control centers.
These colorful tablets can be dangerous in large
doses, especially those which are iron fortified.

♥ Don't give over-the-counter antihistamines to children under the age of two without your doctor's approval. Babies susceptible to sleep apnea are particularly vulnerable to the sedatives in many antihistamines.

♥ Don't take any chances by giving medicine in the dark.

♥ And don't tell your child a certain medicine is "good" or "tastes like candy." It's better to have to struggle a little to get it down than to have your child want more.

If your child does manage to swallow or eat any medicine, get whatever you can OUT of the mouth and call your Poison Control center or 911 immediately. Have the bottle in your hand so you can tell them what was ingested. They will also want to know your child's weight and age. Keep syrup of ipecac on hand, but NEVER use it to induce vomiting unless you are advised to do so. (See page 141.)

Other Bathroom Danger Prevention

♥ Don't leave a sunlamp, hair dryer or other electrical appliance where your child can reach it and pull it into a water-filled tub or sink. Even one that is turned off can cause electrocution if it comes in contact with water. (Some new models can provide protection whether on or off. They have rectangular-shaped plugs with reset buttons at the ends of the cords. As of January 1991 a new voluntary safety standard requires hazard protection in both the on and off positions.) If you use an electric heater in the bathroom, place it high on the wall where your child can't reach it

---

UNPLUG <u>ALL</u> APPLIANCES WHEN NOT IN USE.

♥ Consider installing prong snap-on plug locks to prevent a child from reconnecting an appliance.

♥ Remember to use outlet covers in the bathroom as you do in other rooms. As an extra safeguard against electrocution hazards, install ground fault circuit interrupters (GFCIs) in all wall outlets in the bathroom. (GFCI's can be installed by anyone knowledgeable about house wiring or there are also portable GFCI's that can be plugged into most outlets.)

♥ Put a hook-and-eye catch high up on the outside of the bathroom door so you can keep your child out of the room altogether.

♥ Keep your child from locking himself or herself in the bathroom by attaching door knob covers. You can also drape a hand towel over the top of the

door, or invest in a stopper that fits over the top of
the door. Or put tape across the doorknob bolt so
that it won't close tight. Just in case, keep the key
or an instrument to open the door handy, <u>outside</u>
the room.

♥ Keep scissors and razors locked up as you would
   medicines, and dispose of razor blades safely.

♥ Be as careful to lock up cleaning substances as you
   are medicines. Beauty aids from shampoo to nail
   polish need to be out of reach. They can be poisonous, too!

♥ And remember that some other substances not
   always recognized as dangerous can harm your
   baby if ingested—for example mothballs, liquid
   soap, perfume, and cosmetics. Even good-tasting
   mouthwash, in large quantities, can make a child
   ill.

♥ Use plastic or paper drinking cups to avoid the
   danger of broken glass in the bathroom. Besides, it
   will also prevent the exchange of germs.

♥ A safety gate on a bathroom doorway keeps a child
   out, and if positioned a few inches off the floor
   allows a pet access to a litter box or bowl of water.

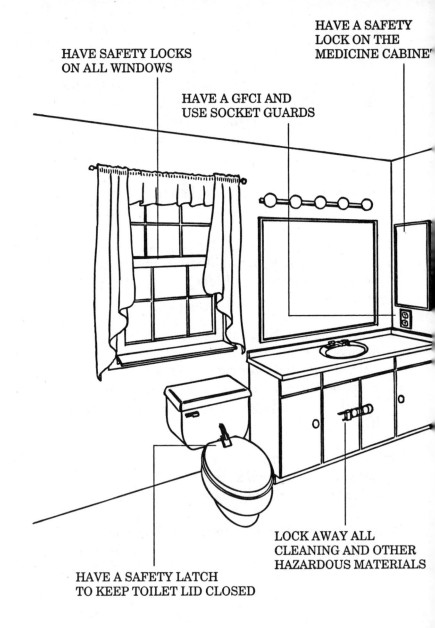

HAVE A SAFETY
LOCK ON THE
MEDICINE CABINET

HAVE SAFETY LOCKS
ON ALL WINDOWS

HAVE A GFCI AND
USE SOCKET GUARDS

LOCK AWAY ALL
CLEANING AND OTHER
HAZARDOUS MATERIALS

HAVE A SAFETY LATCH
TO KEEP TOILET LID CLOSED

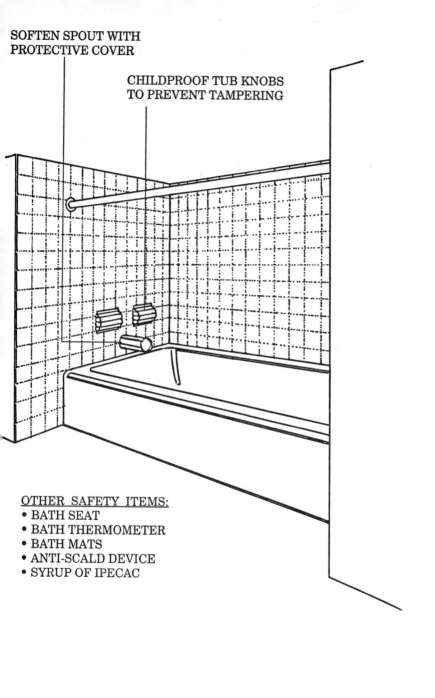

SOFTEN SPOUT WITH
PROTECTIVE COVER

CHILDPROOF TUB KNOBS
TO PREVENT TAMPERING

OTHER SAFETY ITEMS:
• BATH SEAT
• BATH THERMOMETER
• BATH MATS
• ANTI-SCALD DEVICE
• SYRUP OF IPECAC

BABY PROOFING THE NURSERY AND BABY EQUIPMENT

When buying equipment look for the certification sticker of Juvenile Products Manufacturers Association (JPMA). It indicates voluntary safety certification for five common children's items. It ensures that the model has passed rigorous safety standards and is as safe as current manufacturing can make it.

Many products come with vinyl decals bearing the company name or logo. For example, you may see these on a highchair tray or a child's toy. Remove such tags, including JPMA tags, because if your baby manages to get one off, it's a choking hazard. Do, however, leave cautionary and paper warning labels on toys or equipment.

Baby Bassinets, Cribs, Beds and Bumpers

♥ Be sure your bassinet or cradle has a wide base and is sturdy and stable. Don't use a basket not specifically designed as a bassinet. Loose wicker can poke and hurt a baby and the basket may not be stable enough.

♥ Beware, if you buy or borrow a second-hand crib or use an old family one, that it may not meet today's safety standards without modification. For example, the distance between the bars of a crib that ensures a baby can't get his or her head caught is 2 3/8 inches or about the width of three adult fingers, but before 1974, some were set wider apart. There should be at least 12 slats to a crib side. Corner posts should be not more than 5/8 inch above the end boards so they can't catch a baby's clothing and cause strangulation. (The new voluntary standard is that crib corner posts be no more the 1/16 of an inch high to avoid strangulation hazards.) Make sure there are no missing or cracked slots, no decorative cutouts on crib ends large enough to trap a baby's head. Mattress supports should be securely held in the hooks attached to the corner posts. Dropside latches should hold sides securely raised and be difficult enough to operate so that a

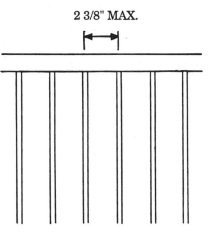

2 3/8" MAX.

small child cannot let the crib side down. All screws and bolts should be tightly in place.

♥ Look for a crib mattress that is non-allergenic, stain-resistant, non-absorbent and anti-static. Be sure that either a crib or bassinet mattress is firm and fits snugly in the crib frame, for the baby's safety as well as comfort. You should not be able to get more than two fingers between the mattress and the crib sides.

♥ Use bumper pads with at least six ties to keep them in place so your baby can't get his or her head between or around them. Be sure the ties are no longer than 12 inches or they become a strangulation hazard. When your child can stand in the crib, it's time to remove the bumpers (as well as stuffed toys or anything else) that can be climbed on. At the same time, adjust the mattress to its lowest setting (the distance from the top of the side rail to the top of the mattress should be at least 26 inches). Some of babies' worst falls occur when they climb out of cribs.

♥ Don't use a pillow for an infant, suffocation can occur if a baby can't raise or turn his or her head. (A pillow will give a one year old or older child practice in "centering" himself or herself—helpful when it is time to move to a big bed.)

♥ Check blankets, to be sure there are no loops or threads to catch a baby's toes or fingers, and comforters to be sure there are no poorly stitched places through which stuffing might escape.

♥ Don't leave rattles, teethers or squeeze-type toys in the crib. They can become wedged in a baby's mouth and cause suffocation.

♥ Avoid placing a crib next to a sash window that cannot be safely (locked) open—thus limiting being lifted from the bottom more than 4-8 inches, and be sure that cords for shades, blinds or lamps are not within reach.

♥ Consider using this rule of thumb: when your child is about 35 inches tall, it's time for a big bed. If it's not possible to move him or her just at that time, put a mattress or a big pillow on the floor beside the crib—just in case.

♥ Never use thin plastic dry-cleaning bags to protect a mattress. They can suffocate a child who gains access to them.

♥ Use a guard rail on the full-size bed until your child is used to sleeping in it, or put a big pillow on the floor beside the bed to break a possible fall.

♥ Never use an electric blanket on the bed of an infant or a child who still wets the bed at night.

Crib Gyms and Mobiles

♥ Don't tie toys across the crib, and don't suspend them on strings from the crib bars.

♥ Check recommended removal times on labels of any crib gyms or mobiles you decide to use. Whatever the recommendation, however, do remove them before your baby can stand, probably at about 5 months, when he or she can push up to hand and knees.

The Changing Table

The Consumer Product Safety Commission estimates that in one year, 1330 children were treated in hospital emergency rooms for injuries related to changing tables. Most injuries occurred when children fell from the changing table to the floor. CPSC knows of nine infants who have died as a result of such falls.

♥ Be sure the changing table you use is sturdily built, with high sides and a safety strap. Keep the strap fastened and, with an active baby, one hand on the child as well, whenever you use the table. Never turn your back on a baby on the table, or leave him or her, even securely strapped down, even for a second.

♥ Keep all diaper-changing supplies out of the baby's reach, and do not keep prescription medicines at the table at all. Be particularly careful with powder. Many containers look much like bottles, and children have actually died from inhaling the powder. Don't give a baby any supply container to play with.

♥ Install an inexpensive, shatter-proof mirror over the changing table at baby's eye level. It will keep the child amused and minimize the chances of him or her squirming out of your grasp.

♥ If you keep a diaper pail near the changing table, be sure it has a locking lid. If it does not, keep it where your child cannot get at it. CPSC has reports of 26 children that have drowned in soaking water and/or been poisoned by diaper pail cake deodorizers.

Infant Seats

Infant seats are wonderful for newborns for <u>almost</u> everything, including eating, playing and napping, but <u>never</u> as substitutes for car seats.

♥ Be sure your infant seat has a wide base, a non-skid bottom and a crotch and waist safety belt.

♥ Beware of placing your baby in an infant seat on a

counter or table. There's a tendency to feel that it's
safe to do so, but it's not.

♥ Do consider setting a baby's infant seat in a playpen
to protect him or her from an older child's atten-
tions.

Infant Swings

♥ Never leave a baby unattended in either an infant
seat or an infant swing.

♥ Use rolled-up towels or cotton blankets to support a
tiny baby in a swing. You can also purchase attractive head support products for infants to use here
and elsewhere.

♥ Be aware that the two most common types of
injuries from swings are: (1) entrapment of a baby's
head when it gets caught between the edge of the
backrest and the bars from which the seat hangs
and (2) falls, when the back of the seat collapses.

Walkers

♥ Check especially for a wide wheel base on your
walker. Coils and hinges should have protective
coverings.

♥ And still, however many precautions you've taken, keep a watchful eye on a baby in a walker.

♥ Let your baby use a walker only on a smooth surface. Even the most well balanced walker can tip over on the edges of carpets or throw rugs or on raised thresholds.

♥ Have a gate securely in place at all open stairwells especially if the walker is used above the first floor. Don't depend upon a pressure gate to keep the baby safe—the force of the walker may dislodge it, and definitely keep doors to open stairways closed.

WALKERS MADE ACCORDING TO JPMA STANDARDS MUST HAVE:

JUVENILE
PRODUCTS
MANUFACTURERS
ASSOCIATION

CERTIFIED

THIS MODEL TESTED BY
AN INDEPENDENT LABORATORY
FOR COMPLIANCE TO ASTM F-977
SAFETY STANDARDS FOR
WALKERS

• A permanent conspicuous label advising that the child should never be left unattended.
• Demonstrated stability against tipping forward, backward or sideways.
• A seating area which keeps the child retained.
• Construction with minimum potential for scissoring, shearing or pinching injuries.
• Holes or openings designed not to catch fingers, toes or buttons.
• A latching device that will prevent the unit from folding accidentally.

Strollers

♥ Don't use a stroller that's not equipped with a safety strap. Many injuries occur because of children not being securely strapped in.

♥ Check to be sure the stroller you buy has a wide, sturdy base and a locking device to prevent accidental folding. Read instructions carefully about folding the stroller and be sure your baby's fingers are out of the way when you open or close it. Practice setting the stroller up and taking it down a few times before you take it out instead of learning how to handle it with a mobile child in tow.

CARRIAGES AND STROLLERS MADE ACCORDINGTO JPMA STANDARDS MUST HAVE:

JUVENILE PRODUCTS MANUFACTURERS ASSOCIATION

CERTIFIED

THIS MODEL TESTED BY
AN INDEPENDENT LABORATORY
FOR COMPLIANCE TO ASTM F-833
SAFETY STANDARDS FOR
CARRIAGES/STROLLERS

* No exposed coil springs that can injure a child.
* Brakes that can't be disengage by a child while he or she is in the stroller or carriage.
* Demonstrated stability on level and inclined surfaces.
* A secure restraining system (except on carriages meant for infants only).

* A latching device that prevents the unit from folding accidentally.

♥ Beware of overloading a hanging diaper bag, purse or package on the stroller handle, especially that of an umbrella stroller. It might tip it over backwards with your child in it. Instead, put a basket lower or at the bottom of a stroller.

Playpens/Play Yards

While you don't want to place your child in a playpen (aka, play yard) all day, as it can inhibit exploration and environmental stimulation, it can be a wonderful containment area when you're cooking or otherwise occupied or when you have to leave a room to answer the phone or go to the door.

♥ Be sure the top rail of the playpen you choose is high enough—20 inches—to keep an 18-month-old child from climbing over it. It should have a firm, cushioned floor.

♥ Measure the holes in a mesh playpen. They should be no larger than 1/4 inch in diameter, so they can't catch buttons on a baby's clothing, toes or fingers.

♥ Never tie a toy across the top of the playpen, it is a strangulation hazard.

♥ Keep the railing of a mesh playpen up tightly; a child can become entrapped in the pocket formed between the floor edge and the mesh siding and suffocate. Unfortunately, this has occurred.

- ♥ Check for sharp edges or protrusions on a playpen, and be sure the locking device will prevent accidental folding.

- ♥ Be sure your child can't lower the dropside of the playpen.

- ♥ Occasionally check vinyl or fabric covered playpen rails for holes or tears. A child may be able to chew off pieces and swallow or choke on them.

- ♥ If you decide to use a portable baby enclosure outdoors, avoid the expandable accordian-style type that forms a continuous circle. The slats cross one another and form large, V-shaped angles at the top and bottom that can trap a baby's neck.

PLAY YARDS/PLAY PENS MADE ACCORDING TO JPMA STANDARDS MUST HAVE:

- • Construction with minimal potential for scissoring, shearing or pinching injuries.
- • Sides with a minimum height of 20 inches from the floor.
- • A strong railing and floor plate.
- • Holes and mesh openings designed not to catch fingers, toes or buttons.
- • A permanent, conspicuous label warning that a play yard should never be used with a dropside in the down position.

Safety Gates

Most safety gates are between 24 and 32 inches tall
and can be adjusted to spaces from about 27 to 42
inches wide. Pressure-mounted gates are easier to
install than those with fixed attachments. But those
with hardware attachments are generally safer for
blocking off stairs or other spaces where security is
most important. (You may find a gate that attaches
only to one side of the opening and can swing open
convenient for a space through which you'll often be
carrying packages or a baby.) Some models offer a
choice of material—plastic, metal or wood.

♥ Examine the size
of the diamond-
shaped openings at
the top of a wooden
accordian-style gate,
if you buy or borrow
a used one. In older
models, these open-
ings are large enough
to catch a child's head
or clothing, while in
newer ones the thick-
er slats and smaller
openings make that

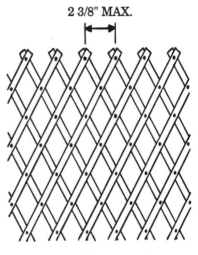

2 3/8" MAX.

impossible. These dangerous gates have not been
marketed since 1985, but, despite fatalities, have
never been recalled.

♥ Check spacing on a bar gate; bars, like those on most cribs, should be no farther apart than 2 3/8 inches to insure that a baby's head can't get caught between the bars.

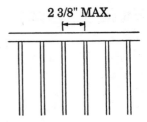

♥ Test the latching mechanism. It should work easily and effectively for you, every time you use it.

♥ Read directions for mounting carefully and be sure the gate is secure when the work is done.

♥ As with other baby equipment, don't rely on a gate to keep your child safe. The one time you're not watching will be the time he or she learns to climb over or around it.

GATES AND EXPANDABLE ENCLOSURES MADE ACCORDING TO JPMA STANDARDS MUST HAVE:

• No V-shaped or accordian shaped openings large enough to entrap a child's head.
• A permanent conspicuous label advising that the child should never be left unattended.
• No splinters, splints, cracks or other defects.
• Openings designed not to catch fingers, toes or buttons.
• Construction that does not allow feet and hands to be caught between that gate or enclosure and the floor or other hard surface.

Around the Nursery

♥ Consider replacing the door of the nursery with a dutch door or screen door so you can see and hear your baby.

♥ Put up in the nursery windows fire rescue decals (such as Tot Spotter or Tot Finder) that will, if necessary, point out the location of a child's room to firemen.

♥ Watch stores and catalogs for attractive smoke alarms designed especially for children's rooms.

♥ Use a UL approved nightlight to help guide you in a dark nursery, but don't put it into a socket near a bed or window where it may touch bedclothes or curtains and cause a fire. Look for one that is a combination outlet cover/nightlight.

The Shared Room

Two major potential safety hazards are present when two young children share a room. The largest is from the older child's toys that can be dangerous to the younger one, either because small parts can be ingested or because many toys for an older child have sharp parts. The second danger is more subtle. Even the most loving and well-intentioned older sibling can act inappropriately with a baby. A room intercom (or baby monitor) can help keep you in touch with activities in the nursery when you're in another room.

♥ Set the crib mattress at its lowest point and leave the crib side up so the older child cannot reach the baby and try to lift him or her out.

♥ Remove any furniture the older child might use to climb INTO the crib.

♥ Explain to your older child why some toys are dangerous for the younger child and enlist his or her help in keeping them in another place in the house.

♥ When the baby becomes mobile and curious, give the older child a feeling of control by supplying locks for a few drawers in which precious (or dangerous) items can be stored.

♥ Put small toys in a tackle box which can be closed and locked by the older child. Also consider wide-mouth, clear plastic jars with screw-on lids.

♥ Avoid the chance of the children being locked in their bedroom. Replace standard doorknobs with the non-locking variety or simply reverse them, so that the lock is on the outside of the door.

♥ Storing an older child's toys on a high shelf and baby toys on lower shelves can work in some cases.

♥ Let an older child play in the baby's playpen with his or her own things.

For children who are not sharing a room, a doorknob cover on an older child's bedroom door helps protect that child's toys from a baby as well as allowing that child to retreat from the baby and play in peace in his or her bedroom. Investing in an additional safety gate for the doorway of an older child's room works well, too. By the time the younger one can climb over the gate, it's probably time to remove it anyway!

Don't entrust the care of a baby to even a responsible, older, small child without an adult available. It's an unfair responsibility to put on the shoulders of a child who can not possibly make a mature decision in all situations that might arise.

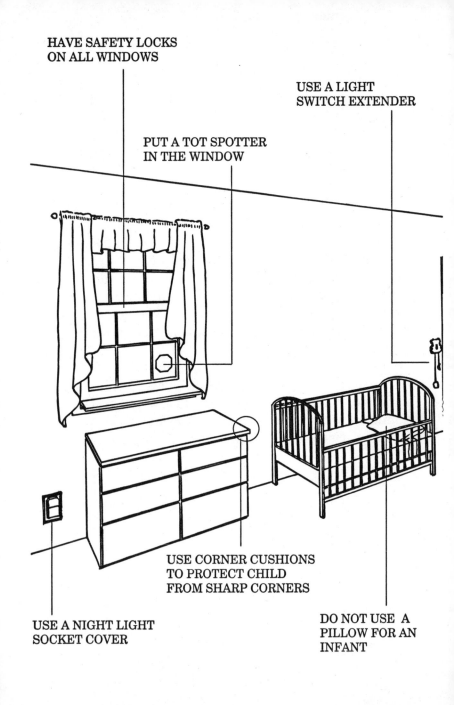

HAVE SAFETY LOCKS
ON ALL WINDOWS

USE A LIGHT
SWITCH EXTENDER

PUT A TOT SPOTTER
IN THE WINDOW

USE CORNER CUSHIONS
TO PROTECT CHILD
FROM SHARP CORNERS

USE A NIGHT LIGHT
SOCKET COVER

DO NOT USE A
PILLOW FOR AN
INFANT

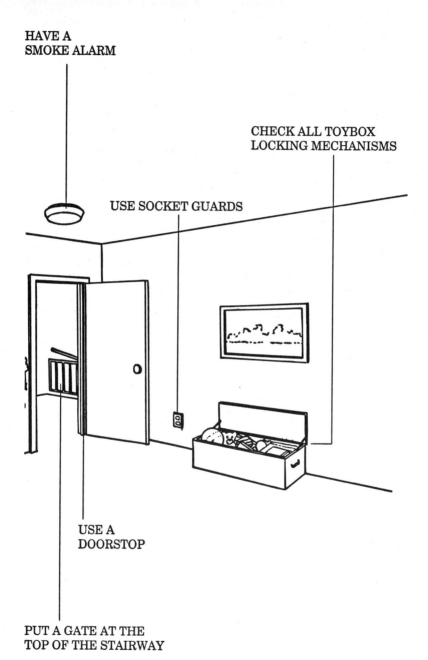

HAVE A
SMOKE ALARM

CHECK ALL TOYBOX
LOCKING MECHANISMS

USE SOCKET GUARDS

USE A
DOORSTOP

PUT A GATE AT THE
TOP OF THE STAIRWAY

THE REST
OF THE HOUSE

Safety-conscious parents breathe a sigh of relief when
they feel the nursery is adequately baby proofed, but
they're not through. They usually find baby proofing
the living room, dining room, family room and bedrooms even more challenging; potential hazards seem
unlimited. Systematic attention to every surface,
every item a baby might be able to reach, is most
important, <u>before</u> it's needed. Empty acessible drawers of anything small, breakable or sharp. Also be
aware and alert to a child's development. The baby
who couldn't pull up last week does it with ease this
week, and the skill of climbing seems to become
routine almost overnight.

Doors

♥ Put decals on sliding glass doors so your mobile
child won't run into them.

♥ Buy a special guard to keep a patio door locked or
insert a spring-loaded curtain rod between the
outside frame and the edge of a sliding patio door,
so your child can't open it and slip out.

♥ Be sensitive to little fingers getting smashed when

closing a sliding door. Consider inserting a small object like a plastic film container so the door can't quite shut all the way.

♥ Put a doorknob cover (a plastic shield covers the knob and slides around on it but doesn't allow the latch to catch) on a door you don't want your child to open, or improvise one by taping an old sock over it. As an extra precaution, attach a bell to the door, so you'll hear if it's opened.

♥ Keep folding doors fully open or completely closed to avoid pinched fingers. Use a door stop on an automatically closing door you want kept open, for the same reason. Watch your child's fingers on the hinges of doors, where they can get caught as easily as between door and door jamb.

♥ Be sure the doors to walk-in closets can be opened from the inside as well as the outside, so no one can get trapped inside.

♥ Attach door stoppers to the tops of doors or to their top hinges. They prevent lock-ins and have the side benefit of preventing pinched fingers if a child puts fingers between the door and the door jam.

♥ Remove door stoppers with rubber caps. These can be removed and eaten by small children, becoming a choking hazard. Replace them with one-piece screw-in door stoppers that attach to the wall, not the door.

Windows

♥ Be aware that any door—front door, bathroom door, basement door—can pose a hazard. Keep them closed.

♥ Install safety glass in large windows and french doors so they won't shatter even if a child falls on them.

♥ Be sure your child won't fall out of a window. Open double-hung windows from the top only or consider using a burglar latch, which will allow the lower sash to open only a few inches. Or install plastic mesh pressure gates securely across lower sashes.

♥ Don't leave furniture or any object that can be climbed upon near a window.

♥ Hang curtains out of your crawling child's reach so he or she can't pull them down.

♥ Tie up the cords to blinds and curtains by clipping them high up with clothespins or wrapping them around cleats mounted high, so your baby can't reach them. Children can wrap them around their necks, creating a strangulation hazard. So be sure drapery cords are either attached to the floor or tied up out of reach.

♥ Use a window lock to safely lock "open" sash windows to a safe height. These locks attach at the top
or side of the window, preventing it from being
opened any further. They can easily be adjusted to
any size opening and don't prevent the window
from closing.

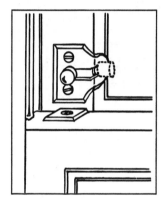

SINGLE POSITION
WINDOW LOCK

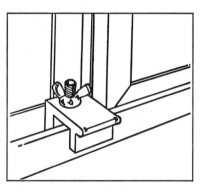

SLIDING GLASS DOOR LOCK

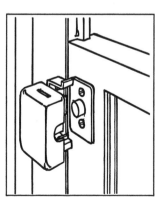

MULTI-POSITION
WINDOW LOCK

Electricity — So Essential, So Dangerous!

Babies and young children seem to be drawn to electricity as steel is to a magnet. They want to poke into outlets, pull and chew on cords and push and jiggle switches—all of which can result in electrical shock and/or serious bruises and contusions. Mouth burns from a child chewing on a plugged in electrical cord is one of the worst hazards. It can take years of corrective plastic surgery to repair such a tragedy. To help you childproof the electrical elements in your home, the Consumer Product Safety Commission offers a free copy of a home electrical checklist in both English and Spanish. Write to CPSC, Electrical Safety, Washington, DC 20207 for a copy.

♥ Cover all electrical outlets that are not in use with safety plugs that snap into outlets. Available also are safety outlet plates for use when a cord is plugged in.

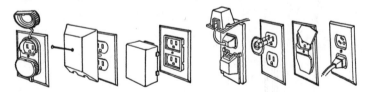

VARIOUS TYPES OF CHILDPROOFING SOCKETS

♥ Check for exposed outlets behind furniture that you have overlooked—but that your child probably will discover.

♥ Don't use extension cords unless absolutely necessary. Be sure any you use are marked #16 or a lower AWG number (the lower the number, the larger the wire and the more current the cord can safely carry). Safety tips on the use of extension cords are available from CPSC. Send a postcard to Cords, CPSC, Washington, DC 20207.

♥ Keep fans up high, out of your baby's reach. The blades are sharp and dangerous, even when the fan isn't operating.

♥ Get all cords completely out of reach of your baby by tacking them under pieces of furniture, taping them to walls or wrapping them around the legs of tables or around cord-shorteners. Telephone cord-shorteners are available and may provide the neatest solutions.

VARIOUS TYPES OF CORD SHORTNERS

♥ Be aware that dangerous overheating can occur if electrical plugs don't fit tightly into wall outlets and if air can't circulate freely around such equipment as television sets, radios, stereos and VCRs. Be sure cabinets enclosing them have proper openings.

♥ If you can't teach your child not to touch those pieces of electronic equipment (some just can't resist!), place them high, if it's possible.

Halls and Stairs

♥ Install one safety gate at the top of a staircase. Use gates you can take down easily so you can let your child practice stair climbing—a necessary skill— when you're able to supervise. And when you do allow practice, teach your toddler to go downstairs backwards, on his or her stomach.

♥ Place the safety gate bar latch on the side away from the child.

♥ Beware of stairs that have open back spaces. A child may be able to squeeze through and fall or get trapped.

♥ Be sure the gaps between upright posts on a stair rail are less than 5 inches, to avoid the chance of your child's head getting caught between them. If gaps are too wide, install plexiglass or a fine, heavy netting along the railing.

♥ Never leave anything on the stairs you can trip on when carrying your baby.

Furniture and Accessories

Don't allow your child to stand or jump on furniture. Not only might a bad fall result, he or she could fall onto another piece of furniture and receive an injury. Several children have actually been killed in such accidents.

♥ Put away, at least for the time being, any unstable or rickety furniture your baby could pull over. Fasten to the wall high bookcases or other pieces a baby might be able to pull down.

♥ Attach small suction cups or small cork blocks to the piano keyboard lid to prevent pinched fingers.

♥ Keep all drawers firmly closed so your baby can't shut fingers in them or climb on them. An esti-mated 2000 hospital-treated injuries in a four-year period were associated with tip-overs of chests of drawers. Consider turning a desk with many inviting drawers to the wall and, for now, storing in the inaccessible drawers papers and small objects you don't need often.

- ♥ When high up and away is not possible, place television sets on low, sturdy furniture, as far back as possible. Tip-overs of TVs on stands, carts and tables are surprisingly common.

- ♥ Move your VCR completely out of reach. It offers great opportunities for injuring hands or fingers. (Not to mention possibilities of ruin if it's "fed" by your child.) Look for new plastic lock shields that protect front loading VCR's.

- ♥ Remove or tighten all loose knobs on furniture or cabinets if they are small enough to swallow (under 1 3/8 inches in diameter).

- ♥ Use wall lamps or ceiling lighting wherever possible, instead of floor or table lamps that a child may be able to pull over on himself or herself.

- ♥ Don't use a cloth on a table in a room a baby will play in. He or she may pull it down, along with everything on the table.

- ♥ Consider putting away your glass-topped table for the time being, or at least cover it with a heavy table pad (and, if it has square corners, plastic corner guards). Children love to pound on any surface, and should your tabletop be broken, dangerous shards could scatter.

- ♥ Buy corner guards and edge cushions for all sharp corners and edges on tables and chests. Many sizes are available to fit various needs. Or tape no longer used shoulder pads or tennis balls cut in half on such corners.

♥ Be aware that recliners offer many opportunities for entrapment of baby fingers and also that children have managed to get their heads caught between the chair seats and leg rests.

♥ Ditto for hideaways beds and all their moving parts.

♥ If you have a separate liquor cabinet or built in bar, be sure it is kept locked.

♥ Keep houseplants out of reach by hanging them instead of using them in floor or table arrangements. Many are poisonous, and it's best not to assume that any are perfectly safe. Keep the name tags of new plants so you'll know what you have, if trouble ever arises. (The most poisonous indoor plants are philodendron, caladium and dieffenbachia. For a list of poisonous indoor and outdoor plants, see page 142.) Symptoms of plant poisoning range from mild nausea and diarrhea to coma but, rarely, death.

♥ Discourage play in the soil around a large plant by covering the top of it with nylon screen from the hardware store. Cut a circle of screen four or five inches larger than the diameter of the pot and slit it from the edge to the center. Slide it around the stem of the plant. Tape or wrap the edges to the pot. Place the pot in a basket or cache pot, the screen won't show and you can water the plant through the screen.

QUICK CHECK LIST

Do you have:
- Any low tables with pointed corners?
- Plants your child can reach?
- An unprotected fireplace?
- Any wobbly furniture that might tip over?
- An unlocked liquor cabinet?
- Accessible electrical outlets?
- Knick knacks, candies, nuts or other mouth-sized items on tables or bookshelves?

Floors, Carpets and Rugs

♥ Avoid thick rugs and shag carpeting; both can harbor such tiny objects as pins, buttons and scraps of food that you don't want to go into your baby's mouth.

♥ Put non-skid backing on scatter rugs so they won't slip out from under your crawling or toddling baby. Don't use scatter rugs at all at the top of staircases.

In Any and Every Room in the House

♥ Be sure paint on walls or furniture doesn't contain harmful amounts of lead which hasn't been allowed since 1978. But many older homes still have heavily leaded paint—especially in undercoats. Peeling paint chips often find their way into the mouths of children—and are still causing lead poisoning today. If you suspect your paint is older than 1980, scrape it off and repaint.

♥ Also be aware that the use of mercury in interior water-based latex paints has been banned by the Environmental Protection Agency. Fumes from the paint have been known to cause mercury poisoning, but the agency has not yet recommended paint removal or repainting. To minimize risk, keep freshly painted rooms aired out. See your doctor if symptoms, including leg cramps, fever and loss of appetite, occur after painting. More information may be obtained by calling the National Pesticide Telecommunications Network, 800-858-7378.

♥ Install smoke detectors in sleeping areas throughout the house and on every floor. Keep fire extinguishers handy in rooms such as the kitchen, where fires are likely to occur.

♥ Put up protective grills in front of fireplaces and always keep a screen before a burning fire. Consider installing the safest "screen"—a heavy glass one. Remove the gas key to a gas fireplace and put it safely away so your child can't accidentally start a fire or let gas fumes fill the room. Be sure your child can't get at the fireplace tools, either.

♥ Use the greatest care with space heaters. Unplug them when not in use and consider using a plug lock to prevent a child from being able to activate one.

♥ Cover hot radiators or make them inaccessible to your baby by placing furniture in front of them.

♥ Never put your baby to sleep on an adult-size bed or waterbed. Over 200 babies have died over the past five years because they suffocated after being entrapped between mattress and wall, bed frame, footboard or headboard or because they were placed in a face-down position. A popular large baby pillow, similar to a beanbag chair, was recently recalled because it, too, was a suffocation threat.

♥ Never set your purse down where your child can get into it. It undoubtedly contains many potentially hazardous items. Likewise, don't leave such interesting items as coins, medicines, pens or jewelry on a dressing table or bureau. Perfume can (and has been) drunk out of the bottle. Children will eat or drink things that taste bad as well as good.

SHOPPING LIST

Corner protectors and edge cushions
Door knob covers
Outlet plugs and covers
Cord shorteners
Cabinet slide locks
Cabinet locks
Door stoppers
Bathtub soft spout
Potty lock
Locking medicine chest
Stove guard, burner guard
Stove knob covers
Refrigerator door lock
Safety straps for all front opening appliances
Safety gates
Smoke detectors
Fire extinguishers

♥ Avoid leaving ashtrays where your baby can get into them and perhaps eat cigarette butts or get a burn from a hot butt. Don't leave matches where a child can get at them to strike or eat them. Children as young as 18 months have been able to operate cigarette lighters.

♥ Keep all kinds of batteries safely out of reach of children. Small button batteries for watches, calculators and cameras usually pass through a child's digestive system, but they have been known to get caught in the esophagus or intestine and leak alkaline electrolytes, causing internal chemical burns.

GARAGES AND WORKSHOPS

The garage and workshop are two areas your baby or young child is best kept out of. Hazardous implements and poisonous substances abound in both. <u>Never</u> work on a car while a child is present. If there'll be other times when your youngster just has to be with you, use every childproofing technique you possibly can.

♥ Never store a discarded refrigerator or freezer in garage or workshop. An empty appliance can become a death trap for a curious child. <u>Any discarded appliance should have its door removed, no matter where it's stored</u>.

♥ Use the same cabinet and drawer guard locks and electrical outlet covers that you use in the rest of the house here, too.

♥ Keep pesticides, plant sprays, car cleaners, paints and other chemicals and supplies, including aerosol cans, locked up. Consider non-toxic alternatives to pesticides and do the environment a favor, as well as yourself. And pay particular attention to safe storage of anti-freeze, because it has a sweet taste.

♥ Don't leave lengths of rope lying about or even hung on walls where a child might reach them.

♥ Store ladders in a horizontal position, so a child cannot try to climb them.

♥ Disconnect power tools after use and consider attaching plug locks to their cords. Insert outlet covers in workshops, too.

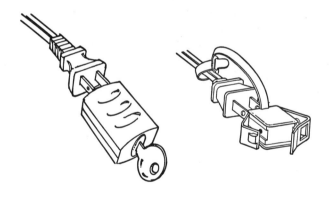

KEY-OPERATED
PLUG LOCK

SELF-ATTACHING
PLUG LOCK

♥ Lock the doors of a car parked in a garage or drive-way. An investigative child might manage to get in and either suffocate from heat or get hurt in dozens of other ways.

Automatic Garage Door Closers

♥ Disconnect and replace a garage door opener that does not reverse when it touches <u>any</u> object. Children who have pushed the switch and tried to run under the closing door have been trapped and killed.

♥ Install the opening switch high on the wall where children can't reach it and keep openers locked up in the car's glove compartment or in a purse.

♥ Never close the door unless you can see that no one is in the way.

♥ Check the door often by closing it on a heavy cardboard box, to be sure the reverse feature is in working order. If it doesn't work, call your door installer!

.2.

Outdoor Safety

You can't childproof the outdoors as thoroughly as you can your house, but you can do a few things to ease your worries. Vigilance is important in your own backyard and even more so away from home.

AH, NATURE!

It's exciting, showing your child all the beautiful and amazing things you've always loved about the outdoors. And it's important to teach respect for nature at the same time you're imparting appreciation, there are dangers that aren't present indoors.

Sun

Start your child very young on a lifetime of protective skin care. While being outdoors is healthy and necessary, too much exposure to direct sun is not.

♥ Keep a baby under a year old out of the hot summer sun altogether, if you can. Dress him or her in lightweight, light-colored clothing and, always, a hat. If you're pushing your baby in a stroller, check often to be sure sun isn't shining directly on his or her face.

♥ Don't use a sunscreen with a sun protection factor (SPF) of 4 or more on a baby under six months old. Tender skin may absorb the chemical involved and be unable to eliminate it.

♥ Do use a sunscreen with a higher SPF on a child, but be aware that anything over 15 may simply be overkill. You may find the ones that come in stick form convenient to use. If in a spray container, spray it on your hands and then apply it to children's exposed skin. Avoid putting it on children's hands—they often end up in the mouth.

♥ Cover all exposed skin surfaces except upper and lower eyelids. Help your child accept the necessity for sunscreen by telling him or her that it's a magic, invisible suit that turns back the harmful rays.

♥ Use zinc oxide if you wish. It offers complete protection for delicate areas such as nose, cheeks and shoulders. And kids love it! It even comes in bright colors today.

♥ Use protection on overcast days, too. As much as 80 percent of the sun's radiation reaches the ground, even through clouds.

♥ Be aware that while a T-shirt will afford some protection (usually about SPF 5) for back and shoulders when dry, once wet, it will only intensify the sun's rays.

♥ Watch your child for signs of heatstroke, if you're out for a long time in hot weather. Most common symptoms are irritability, drowsiness and headache. Get the child into the shade immediately and give cool liquids—water or fruit juice, but nothing with caffeine, because it can lead to dehydration.

Plants in the Wild

♥ Stress the importance of never tasting anything growing in the woods, not leaves, not twigs, not berries, not mushrooms.

♥ Learn what poison oak, poison ivy and poison sumac look like and show your child samples or pictures of all three. Teach the old adage, "Leaflets three, let it be," regarding poison ivy and oak and show your child the familiar sumac shrub or tree, especially recognizable in late summer and fall because of its red leaves. Explain that even just touching these plants can make the skin itch and the mouth burn.

♥ Should your child develop a rash after contact with a poisonous plant, wash the area with soap and water, apply ice or a cool, wet towel and use calamine or a similar lotion to stop the itch.

Bites and Stings

Watch your child for signs of allergic reactions, especially to bee stings. These may include severe itching, nausea, and, more rarely, breathing difficulties and swelling of the throat and tongue. Cover the sting area with a cold, wet cloth to relieve pain, and get your child to an emergency room as quickly as possible. If you know your child is allergic to the stings of bees or other insects, get a medical identification tag for him or her and carry a sting kit.

♥ Choose any commercial insect repellent you use carefully and follow instructions. Avoid the ingredient DEET (diethyltoluamide) or at least avoid repellents with more than 15% DEET because it sometimes causes toxic reactions in children when it is absorbed through the skin. Consider applying such a repellent to your child's clothing. Should your child have a reaction to a repellent, wash the skin with soap and water and call your poison control center or your doctor. Save the container so you'll know the ingredients.

♥ Protect your child with light-colored clothing—long sleeves, long pants and a hat—when he or she will be exposed to mosquitoes or other stinging insects. Discourage the use of perfumes or sweet-smelling lotions by all who will be in your party, and be aware that human beings who are consuming apple juice and other such sweet foods are attractive to insects.

♥ Ease the itch and pain of bites by applying plain white vinegar, alcohol, calamine or another appropriate lotion or cream. Or rub bites with a bar of wet soap or a bit of the liquid from an aloe plant leaf. Amazingly, a paste of meat tenderizer seems to work on some children as does a paste of baking soda.

Lyme Disease

Lyme disease is a bacterial infection spread by a tiny deer tick. The disease, most often contracted during spring and summer, is characterized by a circular red skin rash, fever and chills, nausea and flu-like symptoms such as fever, headache, muscle and joint pain.

Early treatment with antibiotics almost always assures recovery, but it's far better to aim for prevention.

♥ Dress your child in a long-sleeved shirt and long pants, tucked into socks. Don't let your child go barefoot or wear sandals in tick-prone areas. Light-colored clothing will help you spot ticks, tightly-woven fabrics will be harder for ticks to latch onto and burrow into.

♥ Use tick repellent on your child's <u>clothes</u> rather than on bare skin. It's safer and longer-lasting. Repellents with permethrin (Permanone is one) kill ticks on contact, those containing DEET repel the ticks but do not kill them.

♥ Keep your child away from areas of tall grass; walk in the middle of trails when possible.

♥ Check your child's clothes and body for ticks immediately after you get home. Be sure to look in the scalp, too.

♥ Limit the chances of your pets bringing ticks into the house by checking them often and shampooing them frequently with anti-tick soap during the summer months.

♥ For up-to-date information you can contact the Lyme Foundation in Tolland, CT at (203) 871-2900.

IN YOUR OWN BACKYARD

It's as important to baby proof your yard as your house. Of course, your child won't play alone in the yard for some time. Some parents feel that under ideal conditions, including a securely fenced yard with a minimum of hazards, a child of 3 who can be counted on to obey rules set down can be trusted to spend some time outdoors alone, but others wait even longer.

The Play Area

A suitable outdoor play area may be an entire yard, fenced or not, or a part of one. It may be an enclosed deck off the kitchen and should be as carefully baby proofed as a room in your house, where you can watch your child very closely and reach his or her side in an instant.

♥ Check the play and yard areas frequently, watching for broken sidewalks that need repair, loose boards on wooden steps and porches that should be fastened down, holes or ditches in the lawn that should be filled and dangerous litter that should be disposed of, such as broken glass or dog excreta.

♥ Be sure there are no poisonous plants where your child can get at them in the play yard, and pull up mushrooms and toadstools as soon as they appear.

♥ Keep a constant eye on a baby who still puts things in his or her mouth—stones, twigs and dirt are as attractive as rattles or teethers. Better yet, don't put a baby on bare ground.

♥ Install covers or barriers on all window wells around the house.

♥ Install childproof locks on the gate to a fence. And don't leave anything near that a child can climb on to get over the fence.

♥ If your fence is of wood, be sure boards are straight across or curved on top, not pointed.

♥ Lay an extension ladder across the foot of the driveway to keep a young tricycle rider from cruising into the street.

"Sharing" the Play Yard

On occasion, an outdoor play yard will probably become a recreational center for the whole family, and there will always be yard and/or garden work to be done there. It's important to be sure that the adult

equipment and activities don't make the area unsafe
for the kids.

♥ Keep your child out of the area altogether while the
lawn is being mowed. Flying stones and twigs can
cause serious injuries. Never let a child ride with
you on a riding mower.

♥ Don't leave a hose lying in the sun. Water in it can
get hot enough to scald a child.

♥ Fence off trash cans, so an inquisitive child can't get
into them.

♥ String clotheslines high, out of a child's reach, and
be sure there are no dangling cords.

♥ Install ground fault circuit interrupters in any
outdoor electrical outlets as protection against
electrocution hazards.

♥ Get rid of lawn darts, if you have them. They've
been banned since 1988. It's probably best to store
horseshoes and croquet sets, too, until your child is
a little older.

♥ Take the same precautions around a grill and the
outdoor cooking and serving areas that you do in
the kitchen. Keep little kids away while cooking is
going on and remember that charcoal embers stay
hot long after you've finished cooking on them.

Play Equipment

Unfortunately, falls that cause head injuries are real
hazards when children use play equipment. Asphalt
and concrete are <u>not</u> acceptable surfaces to install
under your backyard play equipment. Grass is not
particularly good either, since it wears down and soil
gets very hard-packed. Better "soft" materials are
artificial turf, coarse sand, or layers of pine bark
nuggets. Any such material should be laid to a depth
of 6 to 12 inches, depending on the height of the
equipment, and should extend six feet on all sides
from equipment. Be sure the concrete in which equipment is set is covered completely so children can't trip
and fall on it.

♥ Follow very carefully all assembly instructions for
   equipment you install yourself.

♥ Install non-swinging equipment eight inches and
   swings 20 inches or more from walls, fences, trees
   and other equipment to avoid injury to children
   who fall.

♥ Make regular safety checks all equipment. Look for
   nuts and bolts that are loose or that protrude (those
   that stick up too high can be covered special plastic
   caps). Clamp the ends of S-hooks together with
   pliers so they can't catch a child's skin or clothing
   or allow equipment to come apart. Be sure all wood
   is smooth.

♥ Use nylon, sisal or polyethylene rope for a swing; ordinary hemp rope is not strong enough.

♥ Cover swing chains with sections of garden hose to provide a good grip for a child, and wrap tape around the hose to mark the level at which the child should hold on for best balance.

♥ Teach your child not to twist a swing, whether or not anyone is in it, or to swing an empty swing. Show him or her how to sit safely in the center of the seat, holding on with both hands. And stress the importance of being careful walking either in front of or behind a moving swing.

♥ Be sure the space between the top rung of a play gym's ladder and platform is seven and a half inches, too wide to trap a child's head. If your play gym was produced before 1980, there may not be that much space.

♥ Cover the sandbox when not in use, to keep animals and pets out. Their feces may contain parasites that can harm your child.

♥ Limestone-based sand may contain some asbestos, so it is recommended that when available you buy beach-type, silica based, tremolite-free sand. You can even find this in some chain toystores.

♥ Don't put a bonnet or cap with strings on a child who will play on outdoor equipment. The strings may catch on a chain or knob and your child could be strangled.

♥ Treat a wading pool with the same respect you would a big, in-ground one. Never leave any water in a wading pool not in use. Empty it and either deflate it or turn it upside down.

OUTDOOR PLAY YARD CHECKLIST

• Is the ground surface under equipment covered with "soft" material and are cement anchor blocks completely covered?

• Do you regularly inspect all aspects of play equipment to be sure it's all in safe condition?

• Are you sure there are <u>no</u> spaces of 4 to 8 inches in diameter in which a child's head could get caught?

• Do all the children who play on the equipment understand that it cannot be used in ways for which it was not intended? (No bikes down the slide, for example!)

• Are you prepared to supervise children playing on the equipment and enforce your "house rules"?

THE BACKYARD POOL

A swimming pool in your own backyard offers a
wonderful opportunity for family fun and exercise. It
is also <u>one of the most dangerous single areas
inside or outside your house, since drowning is the
third most common cause of accidental deaths
among children</u>. Parents and teenagers should be
trained (and retrained annually) in cardiopulmonary
resuscitation (CPR). Every year hundreds of children
are saved from drowning because someone at the site
administers CPR immediately. Free courses are
readily available in most communities, and they are
usually completed in a single day. Various pool alarm
systems are available. They're costly, but worth
considering, since one of them may save a child's life.
They include door-exit alarms, fence-gate alarms,
infra-red motion detectors, in-pool alarms that detect
sudden motion in the water and clip-on alarms for
children that sound if water touches the child's skin.

Maintaining clean, bacteria-free water is a
second major concern of pool owners. The best re-
source is a knowledgeable pool service and supply
retailer. Most are members of the National Spa and
Pool Institute. Water should be professionally com-
puter-tested monthly for such characteristics as
mineral content and total alkali and acid quantity,
and weekly, with an inexpensive kit, by the pool
owner. Pumps, filters and other pool maintenance
equipment should be kept in efficient working order.

Remember, KIDS WHO DROWN SELDOM FLAIL AROUND—THEY JUST GO STRAIGHT DOWN. The best precaution against children drowning is to prevent them from falling in.

♥ Fence your pool <u>inside</u> your yard, so it cannot be entered directly from either the house or the play yard. The fence should be at least four feet high (some building codes mandate a minimum of five feet), with spokes or slats not more than 3 inches apart. If you use chain-link fencing, be sure the links are small enough so a child cannot climb on them. Be sure nothing blocks the view of the pool from the house.

♥ A water-activated pool alarm may be needed if the pool is accessible by a door directly from the house.

♥ Put up a child-resistant, spring-lock gate, self-closing and self-latching, with the latch at least 54 inches from the ground.

♥ Install textured concrete or other slip-proof material on the pool deck.

♥ Keep rescue equipment at poolside: a long pole with a shepherd's's crook at one end, at least one ring-shaped life preserver and a long rope.

♥ Put up a CPR techniques poster near the pool (and review it periodically).

♥ Have a phone at the pool so a child won't be left alone even for the moment it takes to answer a call. Keep emergency numbers by the pool phone.

♥ Use only battery-operated radios or television sets near a pool. If you <u>must</u> have an electrical appliance of any kind in the pool area, be sure the outlet is protected by a ground fault circuit interrupter (GFCI).

♥ Install a safety line where water deepens to a point your child should not go beyond.

♥ Get an approved safety pool cover that will support at least 30 pounds of weight per square foot. Look for one that complies with ASTM safety standards. Fasten the cover securely during the non-swimming months of the year, being sure there are no gaps that will allow a child to slip through. Remove the cover completely before anyone enters the water.

Pool Safety Rules

Supervision is most adequate when it's on a one-to-one basis between children and adults. Make up your own set of inflexible pool rules and insist that everyone, child or adult, guest or family member, follow them. Rules number one and two should be that there is no running around the pool and no roughhousing.

♥ <u>Never,</u> <u>never</u> leave a child in the pool alone. In fact, don't take your eyes off the child. Drowning can occur in a matter of seconds.

♥ And don't drink alcoholic beverages while you are watching children. You can't afford to have your reflexes impaired.

♥ Don't take a baby in a pool before he or she has good head control (can lift head to a 90° angle). There's the possibility that the head of a baby under about five months may accidentally bob under water.

♥ Don't allow a child under five in a spa or hot tub. Children's lighter body weight and developing organs make them more sensitive to stress from high water temperatures.

♥ Don't trust "drown-proofing" or swimming lessons to protect your child. Twenty-five percent of the children who drown have had at least some lessons. Panic can overtake even a good swimmer under some situations.

♥ And don't rely on any of the various inflatable flotation devices available to keep your child safe. Most can be punctured or deflated and are not designed to keep a child's head above water. They "work" under ideal conditions, but can give both you and your child a false sense of security. Your vigilance is all you can trust.

♥ Don't submerge an infant's face. It's true a baby will automatically hold his or her breath, but swallowing will continue, and large quantities of water ingested can dilute the blood and lead to water intoxication and other problems.

♥ Never allow ride-on wheel toys of any kind in the pool area. Don't leave toys or other objects in the pool when you're through for the day. Your child may be attracted to them and try to go after them.

♥ Get everybody out of the pool immediately at the first sign of a thunderstorm.

AT THE BEACH

Most of the safety rules that apply in a backyard swimming pool apply at the beach, plus a few others. The combination of sand and water can intensify the effects of the sun, so be aware that rays are most intense between the hours of 10 a.m. and 2 p.m. (11 a.m. and 3 p.m., Daylight Saving Time) and take special pains with protective measures on children.

♥ Be sure plenty of drinking water is available for everyone at the beach. Toddlers and preschoolers love having their own canteens.

♥ Check the lake or seashore bottom to be sure there aren't sharp stones or shells to cut your child's feet. Sneakers may be good protection anytime.

♥ Don't underestimate the strength of the gentlest looking waves. A small wave, plus just a slight undertow, can be disastrous for a light and perhaps unsteady child.

♥ Show your child a jellyfish, when you see one, and explain why it should not be touched. If your child is stung by one, wash the area with sea water and apply a baking soda paste. Hydrocortisone cream and antihistamines will relieve burning and swelling.

♥ Look into various products that offer shade for a baby if you're at the beach often—several styles of "cabanas" and covered strollers are available.

♥ Or keep a baby both off sand and out of the sun by turning a playpen upside down on a sheet to make a cool shady "cave."

Boating

The safety of the passengers is the responsibility of the skipper, be they on an ocean liner or in a small outboard boat. If a baby or young child is among the passengers, the responsibility is obviously heavier than in a boatload of accomplished swimmers.

♥ Don't let any passengers, especially children, sit on the tops of seats, the gunwales or the bow. A person who falls from the bow is very likely to be hit by the propeller of an outboard motor.

♥ Be sure that <u>all</u> small children (along with any other non-swimmers) wear properly put on personal flotation devices (PFDs) all the time the boat is in the water, and that PFDs are readily available for all others in the boat. (Some parents feel safer if children wear life jackets whenever they play on a shore near water.) Be sure the PFD you select is comfortable. Kids, especially, will fight wearing life jackets that are uncomfortable.

♥ Have your child try the PFD in the water, to allow both you and him or her to see how it actually works. Its real purpose is to float an individual, keeping both head and mouth out of the water. If it doesn't work, return it!

CAMPING AND HIKING WITH KIDS

It's not only possible to have your baby or small child join you in camping and other outdoor activities, many parents have found, but also great fun. The magic words to act on are "plan carefully" and "expect the unexpected."

♥ Watch your baby or young child constantly. Don't appoint an older child as babysitter—there is no substitute for your own careful and experienced supervision at the campsite. Attach a bell to the child's clothing so you can hear as well as see him or her.

♥ As an extra precaution, put an identification tag on your child. A luggage tag will work well. Include the child's and your name, campsite number, auto license number and pertinent medical information.

♥ Keep fishing gear up and away where your child can't possibly get into it. A sock, hung high on a tree where a child can't reach it, makes a good container for fishhooks, matches and other small items.

♥ Don't let your child drink from a stream, however clear and clean it may look. If you wish, put some of the water in a container and purify it with special tablets.

♥ Don't allow your child to touch a wild animal or bird, even when dead. Rabies is only one of the possibilities of infection. If your child is bitten by a wild animal, wash the wound carefully and see a doctor. Try to confine the animal so authorities can check it, if that's not possible, at least try to identify it.

♥ For hiking, stick to a front carrier for your baby
until he or she is five to six months old. The necks
of children younger than that aren't strong enough
to withstand even minor jolts.

♥ Remember to bend from the knees when your child
is in a backpack, to keep him or her from falling
out.

BIKING

Don't carry a baby under six months of age on your
bike. And never use a front- or backpack as a bike
carrier; neither are safe for this purpose. Use a well-
made, sturdy carrier that mounts on the <u>back</u> wheel
of your bike.

Carriers and Helmets

As with other baby and child equipment, it's not
always a good idea to try to save money by buying
bargain or used carriers Parts may be missing and
there will probably not be proper instructions for
installation or use.

♥ Mount the special child carrier firmly and properly
on the rear wheel of your bike. Be sure the carrier

has an adequate safety harness that restrains both the upper and lower parts of your child's body, a high back and shields for the child's feet.

♥ A child riding in a bike carrier should wear a helmet. Buy yourself and your child good helmets that meet ANSI (American National Standards Institute) standards. Kids' helmets come in sharp colors, and some have special decal decorations. You can approach the subject of wearing a helmet as you do that of the car seat: it's automatic; you just do it!

♥ Make yourselves more visible by attaching a fluo-rescent warning flag to the carrier, and improve your own vision of the road with a rearview mirror.

Rules of the Road

♥ Ride on bike paths or lightly-traveled streets. On the road, stay to the right, going <u>with</u> the traffic.

♥ Use hand signals to clearly indicate your turns to drivers around you.

♥ If several of you are riding together, travel in single file as you pass others on a bike path. And for safety's sake, always ride single file in the street.

.3.

Traveling About

Around the neighborhood, around the country, around the world. On foot, by bike, by auto, by plane. Off you go with your baby, ready for new experiences. The better your planning and the more conscious you are of safety, the happier those experiences will be for both you and your child.

GOING BY CAR

Motor vehicle accidents are the leading cause of death for young children. (*Read that sentence again.*)

Children properly restrained have a 70% greater chance of surviving an accident. (*Read that sentence again!*)

```
SAFETY SEATS SAVE LIVES
```

Car Seats

For safety's sake (and by law, in all states) babies and children <u>must</u> ride in crash-test, child restraints— not in your lap, not in a portable crib or car bed. Again, parents are advised not to save money by picking up a used car seat at a garage sale. The model may be obsolete; it may have been recalled and not repaired or it may have been used in a crash. The label on a car seat should indicate that the seat meets all applicable Federal Motor Vehicle Safety Standards (FMVSS) and has been manufactured after January 1, 1981.

There are three basic kinds of car restraints. The infant-only seat is for babies from birth to nine months or 20 pounds. It is to be used semi-reclined and must be placed <u>facing backwards and in the back seat only</u>. Make sure it is tightly secured with a safety belt and the baby is buckled into the re-straint. A convertible car seat is for a child from birth to 40 pounds. If used for a child under 20 pounds, position it like an infant-only seat. When your child is a year or older or over 20 pounds, it should only be used in the upright position, facing forward and placed in the safest place—the back seat of the car. Then there are booster seats (the shield type and the belt positioning booster) which elevate a child who has outgrown a standard safety seat but still isn't tall enough to fit the adult belts. These work in conjunction with the car's safety belt system, but the belt-positioning type works in conjunction with a combination lap/shoulder belt. Wait until your child is at least 40 pounds and has really outgrown the convertible car seat before using a booster seat.

An auto booster seat can double as
a booster seat in a restaurant, etc., but
A HOUSEHOLD BOOSTER SEAT SHOULD
NEVER BE USED AS A CAR BOOSTER SEAT.

♥ Support a tiny infant by placing rolled towels, diapers or receiving blankets on either side of the safety seat to keep the head from falling side to side. Or purchase an infant head support.

♥ Don't dress your baby in so many clothes that the car seat can't be used properly. Use outfits with legs so the harness will fit snug to the body. Cover him or her with a blanket after hooking up, if necessary.

♥ Make sure, if you borrow a seat, that it has not restrained a child in an accident. The structure of the seat may have been weakened. Replace your own safety seat if it has been in an accident.

♥ Explain the necessity for using a car seat to your child, as well as insisting that it be worn. He or she should eventually come to understand not only that it is important, but also why it is important.

♥ Give your take-charge child a feeling of control by allowing him or her to hook up the car seat, but you check to be sure it's done right. Straps should fit snugly, too.

♥ Try to find a seat that allows your child to see out the car windows to help reduce boredom. But don't install the seat so close to windows or doors that their controls can be reached—the center of the back seat is best.

♥ Cover the safety seat with a blanket or towel, when the car is parked outdoors, to keep the vinyl cover from getting too hot or too cold. Or get a lambskin seat cover, which will keep the seat warm in winter, cool in summer. Always test the seat's metal and plastic parts with your hand or wrist before putting a child into the seat.

♥ Get roller shades for the windows in the back to protect a child in a car seat from bright sun.

♥ Be prepared to leave your safety seat when you leave your baby with grandma and grandpa, or any caretaker who will be transporting your child. Or you can also switch cars to avoid the inconvenience of moving car seats around. Just be sure your child is always in a car seat when in transit.

Your community or car insurance company may offer a "loaner program" for car seats. For information on a program in your area, contact your state highway safety program.

The National Highway Traffic Safety Administration is the federal agency in charge of auto, highway and pedestrian safety. It provides information on safety belts and children's car seats and other safety matters. If you do choose a previously used seat, you may wish to make sure it is not one that has been recalled. To report a safety defect, get recall or other information, write the Department of Transportation, Dept. NEF 10, Washington, DC 20590 or call their Auto Safety Hotline, toll free, at 800-424-9393 (In DC, call 366-0123).

For special help to specific questions about how to use and install your specific car seat, you also can call SafetyBeltSafe U.S.A. at 213-673-2666.

Installing a Safety Belt Correctly

Read the instructions for installing the safety seat correctly and at the location specified by the manufacturer.

Be sure the vehicle belt is routed through the seat in the right way. A third or more of the nation's car seats are installed incorrectly, it is said, so double-check yours. Read the vehicle owners manual for special instructions, especially if your car has automatic, motorized, passive safety belts or air bags.

Be aware that some safety seats simply can't be properly installed in some cars; check for compatibility before you buy. In some cars, the safety belt can't be made tighter on the safety seat You may need a locking clip. In general, the belts that have large buckles do not require clips; if the buckle slides easily along the belt, you may need one. If you think you need a locking clip, or don't know, contact SafetyBeltSafe USA or the motor vehicle manufacturer.

Rules of the Road

♥ Make "Hands up!" the first rule. Everyone in the car raises hands to show they're out of the way before the car doors are shut.

♥ Make a rule that the engine isn't started until everyone is safely restrained.

♥ Insist on the basics from the beginning: no throwing anything in the car; no grabbing the steering wheel or keys; no playing with door locks or window buttons.

♥ Pull over and stop the car if children scream or fight, and don't start up again until quiet reigns.

♥ Carry any heavy or sharp object in the trunk, not on the dashboard, back shelf or anywhere else loose in the car. It could become a deadly missile in a quick stop or accident.

♥ Get in the habit of checking under and behind your car before backing out of your driveway.

Pleasant, Convenient, and SAFE

♥ Prepare to use incentives to get children to behave well, in order to make a long ride safe and pleasant. Enjoy family singing and games and play the kids' favorite tapes. Bring a bag or box of soft, safe toys for each child and lap boards or cake boxes with lids to play on.

♥ Never allow lollipops or ice cream bars on sticks in the car, and avoid drinks that require straws. In a sudden stop or accident all become real hazards.

♥ Be careful about any food you do let children eat as
  you travel. Choking can pose a special danger in a
  car as the driver may overreact to the situation,
  turning a brief scare into a tragedy.

♥ Store the knife you use for cheese or fruit in a round
  toothbrush holder that closes tightly so a child can't
  get at it.

♥ Consider traveling at night or very early in the
  morning, so children will sleep for part of the trip.
  Don't let children lie down to sleep, though. Have
  them lean sideways against the side of the car,
  supported by big pillows, if they can't simply lean
  back in car seats and doze.

♥ Get a small, wide-angle mirror to clip to the front
  seat visor or attach to the windshield with suction
  cups so the driver or another adult can monitor a
  child in a car safety in back. Also available is a
  plastic "mirror" that adheres to the back window
  of a station wagon or van and gives a 180° view of
  what's behind.

Parking

♥ <u>Never</u> leave a child unattended in a parked car,
  even for a moment, risking abduction or serious
  injury from heat buildup. At an outside temperature of 85°, the temperature in a car with the

windows slightly open will rise to 102° in 10 minutes.

♥ On a city street, try to park where your child can be lifted out on the sidewalk side of the car, away from traffic.

♥ Make an inflexible habit of turning the car motor off and removing the keys every time you park, whether or not there are children about.

♥ Walk around a parked car before getting in and starting it to be sure there are no children near it.

GOING SHOPPING

A fairly recent concern for some parents is that of environmental dangers. Try to avoid traffic jams that cause pollution by choosing less busy times to go out in the car, and if you're caught in heavy traffic, close the car windows and turn on air conditioning, if possible. If you live in the city, and especially if your child has asthma or other lung problems, avoid walking very far on crowded streets in hot, muggy weather if you can.

♥ Set a small baby in his or her infant seat, propped up in the grocery cart seat. Or in one of the small basket carriers supermarkets supply, with blankets to keep him or her steady. Some infant-only safety seats have special clips for attachment to shopping carts.

♥ Carry with you a safety strap for a child who can sit in the seat, so he or she can't stand up and fall out. Falls from shopping carts are among the leading causes of head injuries to children treated in emergency rooms.

♥ Take your baby on mall shopping trips in either a backpack, which has the advantage of leaving your hands free, or in a stroller. If your child insists on walking, use a harness.

♥ Hold your baby on an escalator; it's mandatory. Holding any child you can lift is safest.

♥ Don't let your child wander about a store, touching and handling merchandise. Besides annoying shopkeepers and possibly breaking something you'll have to pay for, the child may injure himself or herself on something sharp or otherwise harmful.

♥ Do not let your child go to a restroom alone until he or she is about six years old. Only let a child go alone when you are familiar with the place, know it is clean, and can see the door plainly.

Traffic

It's important to begin teaching your child "street smarts" early. As you cross streets and move through town with your baby, talk about how you're obeying laws and observing safety rules even if you're not sure he or she can understand you yet.

See the road from your child's point of view by dropping to your knees on a street corner and trying to judge car speeds and distances. Remember that children have a third less peripheral vision than adults, as well as less height.

♥ Don't take a toddler into traffic without some way to hold on to him or her securely. Holding hands is one way, and some children can be depended upon to hold on to an adult's coat or a stroller. Safest of all is pushing the child in a stroller or using a harness with reins. (An attractive, comfortable harness makes a child feel secure and allows you the peace of mind that comes from knowing he or she can't come to harm!).

♥ Always use an official street crossing, even when it's more time-consuming to do so, and explain why you're doing so to your child. Talk about the dangers of crossing in the middle of a block, and especially those of going into the street between parked cars.

♥ Stop at the curb, and look not just <u>both</u> ways, but left, right and then left again. Children can't always tell if a car is moving the first time they see it. Listen as well as look, and continue to do both as you cross.

♥ Walk briskly, but don't run, and explain to your child that the reason for this is that the possibility of tripping and falling is greater if you're running.

♥ If you walk on city streets at night, put reflective clip-on patches, tape or clothing on yourself as well as your children.

GETTING THERE BY AIR

Currently, children under 2 may ride on most airlines free, but they are required to be held in their parents' laps during takeoff, landing or emergencies. If you wish to guarantee a seat for a child under 2 because you plan to use a safety seat, you will need to purchase a ticket for that child. But buying a seat for an infant or toddler has not up to now ensured that a parent could put the child in a car seat aboard the plane seat. Airlines have not had a uniform policy on

the use of such restraints, but changes in these
practices may come soon. You will find that airlines
won't let you use such a safety seat in emergency
access rows, in the rows just in front and back of
them, and probably in an aisle seat. The National
Transportation Safety Board has recommended that
separate safety seats be required on airliners for
children. Not agreed upon are details such as who
would provide the seats and whether full or partial
fare would be required for the children.

- ♥ Keep your child in a stroller or put a harness on
  him or her in the airport. Crowds and confusion
  have contributed to the separation of many a
  parent and child, causing unnecessary panic and
  often serious delays.

- ♥ For good measure, outfit your child with a travel
  bracelet or hang on him or her a luggage tag with
  both the child's and parents' names, the home and
  vacation addresses and telephone numbers and
  any important medical information.

- ♥ At takeoff, and especially on landing, give your
  child something to suck on to help overcome pressure on ears. For an infant, breastfeeding or a
  bottle is best; a pacifier will serve the purpose.

- ♥ Don't drink a hot beverage when flying with a child.
  Chances it can spill are good, and your child, as
  well as you, could receive a bad burn.

VISITING GRANDPARENTS AND OTHERS

The duration of a visit will determine the amount of childproofing of another's house you'll feel necessary. A short afternoon visit during which you and child are together in the same room all the time requires little except your vigilance. On the other hand, for everyone's peace of mind during a long stay at Grandma's, more serious childproofing efforts will be worthwhile. And if Grandma lives close and you stop in often, you'll want to encourage her cooperation or do your own childproofing at her house.

Good to Carry With You

♥ You can't carry with you every conceivable childproofing product you might want during a long or short visit, but a few items in a small bag will ease your mind when you're visiting a totally un-childproofed home.

♥ Bungi cords, two or three, with which to secure kitchen or bathroom cabinets and/or drawers in certain pieces of furniture. Perhaps a packet of long pipe cleaners as well, for some kinds of cabinet closures.

♥ Outlet covers, at least a dozen.

♥ Doorknob covers, two or three, with which to keep your child out of rooms that contain dangerous items.

♥ An intercom, which will allow you to check on a child sleeping in a distant room.

♥ Syrup of ipecac or activated charcoal, in case your child swallows something poisonous and you are advised by the poison control center to administer it.

At Grandma's

♥ Ask Grandma to prepare for your visit be doing a little childproofing, or do it yourself. Help her out by giving her a gift of some childproofing items such as latches, outlet covers and doorknob covers. In a pinch, tape can be used to cover outlets.

♥ Be especially sure that grandparents' medications are locked up safely; they may not have childproof caps and thus be extra hazardous. (And when grandparents visit you, ask that their medicines be locked into suitcases.)

♥ Check to see that outdoor areas are safe for your child. Be sure that a garage door closure that doesn't stop the door when it comes in contact with any object is disconnected.

♥ Put a list of emergency numbers by Grandma's phone, including that of the local poison control center.

♥ If grandparents will be driving your child around, either move your child's car seat to their car or, perhaps easier, trade cars with them.

Eating and Sleeping Away from Home

♥ Carry your own restraint system for restaurant highchairs; many don't have safety straps. Carry it also for a visit to a home where a highchair you haven't seen will be provided, just in case.

♥ When attaching hook-on highchairs, be careful they are not near anything on which a child can get leverage to dislodge the chair. Don't use a hook-on chair on glass, loose-top or pedestal tables, or with placemats or tablecloths. Use hook-on chairs only as they are designed to be used, with restraining straps, and only until your child weighs not more than 30 pounds, even though they're tested to hold more.

♥ Check your child's sleeping arrangements carefully. A borrowed or rented crib may not meet all the safety standards the one you use at home does. If a travel bed or playpen is substituting for a crib, be sure it is set up correctly and does not present special hazards. For your own peace of mind and your baby's comfort, consider investing in a safe, convenient port-a-crib.

♥ Carry a UL approved nightlight with you when you travel, so you can safely tend your child in the night.

.4.

Safety in Play

Play is your child's "work" and toys and art materials are the learning tools necessary for his or her development. Unfortunately, many toys are unsafe and some art materials contain dangerous toxins. Every year, about 125,000 children at play are injured seriously enough to be taken to emergency rooms. Thus vigilance is called for in the "fun" area as well as in the ordinary realities of everyday living. It's not possible for you to know too much about potential dangers or to inspect too carefully anything with which your child will play.

TOYS

The main causes of injuries from toys are small parts that are swallowed or choked on, sharp edges and points that cut or puncture and loud noises that impair hearing. Parents should avoid toys with such features and should also remember that any toy must be safe for a baby or toddler to "mouth." That means it's probably safe if: it's too large to be swallowed, it's not sharp enough to cut the child's lips or mouth and it does not have any pinch points that might catch tongue or lips.

There's a temptation to accept the word of a toy manufacturer who claims a toy is "safe" or "non-toxic," but these terms are sometimes vague. Remember, too, that seals of approval from organizations are not guarantees of safety. It's also useful to know that while the Consumer Product Safety Commission recalls products it deems dangerous, not every toy that has been implicated in a fatality has been recalled. And those recalled do often show up at garage sales and as family hand-me-downs.

A firm and inflexible rule that should be enforced from the beginning is that toy throwing is an absolute no-no. Balls may be rolled between children and adults or between kids old enough to have mastered that skill, but even soft toys must not be thrown. Children too young to understand and observe the rule should be separated if they throw toys at each other.

Baby Toys

At least sixteen children's deaths in the United States
are attributed to baby rattles, according to CPSC
reports. The victims either partially swallowed rattles
while sucking on them or fell with rattles in their
mouths, causing them to be jammed into their
throats. Squeeze toys and teether toys have been
involved in similar choking incidents. Over the years
baby toys have vastly improved given these concerns,
but they still don't have to be certified as safe. Infants'
mouths and throats are extremely flexible and can
stretch to hold larger shapes than one might expect,
the largest on record being a rattle with an end 1 5/8
inches in diameter.

♥ Check the size of <u>handles</u> and <u>ends</u> of rattles,
   squeeze toys and teethers to be sure they aren't
   small enough to lodge in a baby's throat and
   obstruct the airway.

♥ Remove rattles, squeeze toys and teethers from the
   crib or playpen when your baby sleeps.

♥ Be sure when you buy them that toys can be easily
   cleaned, because for a long time your baby' primary
   way of playing with them will be to suck or chew
   them, and you'll want to wash them often.

♥ Check rattles and other baby toys to be sure they
   don't have seams that might come apart, separat-
   ing the item into sharp or dangerously small pieces.

Pacifiers

♥ <u>Never</u> allow a pacifier to hang on a string or ribbon around a baby's neck. Attach it instead on a <u>short</u> string or ribbon (not longer than 7 inches) pinned to the shoulder of a child's shirt or dress. Or buy a commercially made pacifier holder that pins or clips to a child's clothing.

♥ Check any pacifier you buy to be sure it is produced according to current requirements. It must be strong enough not to break into small pieces, have guards to keep it from being drawn into a child's mouth and have ventilation holes to allow the child to breathe even if the guard gets into his or her mouth.

♥ Check the condition of pacifiers regularly for deterioration. Discard any that seem weakened or that have changes in texture, tears or holes. Boil pacifiers for a few minutes occasionally, to avoid infection and re-infection with diseases such as colds, flu or thrush.

Toy Chests and Containers

♥ The best storage for toys is low, open shelves on which your child can see and reach everything easily. Be sure they're mounted low enough so the child doesn't have to climb to get at a toy.

♥ Check whatever shelves, chests or containers you may use for sharp corners and rough edges.

♥ Remove a heavy, free-falling lid on a toy chest so it cannot cause head or neck injuries. Putting good-sized cork or wooden blocks on all four corners prevents lids from slamming on little fingers. The lid should have spring-loaded supports to hold it open at any level—if it doesn't, buy them and attach them to the chest. Better yet, look for a chest that opens with sliding panels.

♥ Be sure there is ventilation in any chest or toy storage box large enough for your child to fall or crawl into.

Reading Labels on Toys

Labels are helpful and will tell you a great deal, but in buying toys, as in every other phase of child-rearing, your own common sense and good judgment should be the last words.

♥ Pay attention to the age recommendations on toy labels, but be aware that they're only estimates and won't be accurate if your child is developing more or less rapidly than the "average" child. You should also know that some toys are advertised and marketed towards children younger than the age on the package indicates.

♥ Remember that a toy suitable for a 6-year-old may be totally unsafe for a 3-year-old. Problems arise when an older and a younger child share a room or play together. (See page 37.)

♥ Don't try to "challenge" your child by buying a toy recommended for an older one or because you think he or she is brighter than average. Both physical and mental development must be considered, and a child advanced enough physically to handle a particular toy may not be mentally or psychologically capable of dealing with it. Such toys may contain small parts that will be dangerous for a younger child.

♥ Be aware that while "non-toxic" on the label does guarantee that chewing a toy won't fatally poison a child, it does not guarantee it won't make a child sick if ingested. It only guarantees the child won't be fatally poisoned.

♥ Read all the fine print on a label; there may be disclaimers or conditions that you need to weigh. "Safe for use with adult supervision," for example, may, in your judgment, mean not safe at all for your baby.

Toys to AVOID for Babies and Little Kids

Don't give your child:

Toys that have small parts that can be swallowed or become lodged in a child's windpipe, ears or nose, such as doll accessories, small snap-together blocks or beads or puzzles with small pieces. CPSC has developed the "truncated cylinder test tube," now available in retail stores. This clear plastic tube allows things to fall through it that are too small to give a child under 3 years of age (but items marked for children 3 and over do not have to pass this test). Don't rely completely on such "rules of thumb." Children from one month to 4 years old have choked on products that passed the commission's safety tests. Be aware that the worst offenders are pieces of broken balloons that children ingest and the marbles and small balls that often come in games.

PASS

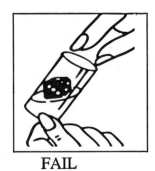

FAIL

BROKEN TOYS ARE DANGEROUS TOYS

Call CPSC (800-638-CPSC) to report
an unsafe toy or one that has caused an accident.

Rocking Horses

♥ Be sure that a rocking horse is attached securely to
its base. Check for all over sturdiness and for flaws
such as sharp edges or uncovered springs.

♥ Cover rods that serve as handles and pedals on a
rocking horse with bicycle grips or rubber tips
made to cover chair legs.

Riding Toys

♥ Be sure any riding toy you buy has wheels widely
spread for stability. Pedals and hand grips should
have rough surfaces and treads to keep a child's
hands and feet from slipping.

♥ Be aware that while the popular vehicles with low-
slung seats close to the ground are extra stable,
they also make the rider less visible. Fatalities
have occurred when they were ridden or rolled into
streets. If your child does have one, be sure to
attach a flag to it's wheels to make it more visible.

♥ Don't buy a riding toy with seams that go around wheels. The seams can split and cause an accident.

♥ Avoid battery-powered riding toys for little kids. Even though they travel only at two to four m.p.h., tipping can still occur and they are unsafe.

♥ Match the size of any riding toy or tricycle to the size of the child. If the child is too large, the toy or tricycle will be unstable; if the child is too small, it will be difficult for him or her to control.

♥ Start a child out on a first tricycle with a helmet. Always wearing one is a good practice to establish for later bike riding.

♥ Don't leave a tricycle out at night. Moisture causes rust that will weaken metal parts.

ARTS AND CRAFTS

Creativity is exciting for kids but not without it's safety concerns for parents.

Though your child of 3 or under is not quite ready to turn out much in the way of art work, he or she should be given the opportunity to scribble and paint on big sheets of paper, to squeeze and pummel clay and, at about 2 or so, to begin to paste and cut.

Buying the Supplies

Toxins in some art materials may be dangerous for small children, especially if they're ingested. They can also be absorbed through the skin or inhaled. Some potentially dangerous products have not been so marked, but a federal law requiring a hazard label is scheduled to take effect late in 1990. Look for products with CP (Certified Product) or AP (Approved Product) or HL/NT (Health Label/Non-Toxic) seals. They do not contain materials in sufficient quantities to be toxic or injurious to children.

♥ Buy simple and inexpensive art materials for your child in reliable stores. Start with only a few basics; little kids don't need and won't appreciate great quantities of sophisticated materials. Finger paint, jumbo wax crayons, washable markers, poster paint or powder paint you mix yourself with water, dustless chalk, and inexpensive clay or Play Doh™ are good for beginners.

♥ Avoid oil-based products that contain dangerous solvents, aerosol spray paints, solvent-based inks and permanent or scented markers. Opt instead for water-based products.

♥ Buy white glue or school paste, not airplane glue or rubber cement.

♥ Buy <u>big</u> painting brushes (not artists' brushes) in a hardware store—look for short ones, too wide to fit into a small mouth.

Getting Down to Work

Supervise! Don't leave your child alone with art materials both to keep him or her from harm and to protect your house!

♥ Keep your child engaged in art work in one place. The kitchen may be the ideal room. A highchair is great for a toddler; an older child can work at a table with a washable surface or stand up at an easel.

♥ Help your child of 2 or 3 learn to cut with safe children's scissors—blunt and sized for a child's hand. Buy left-handed scissors for a left-handed child. They will be safer, because he or she will be able to handle them better.

♥ Let children from toddler-age to preschooler paint your house or driveway, in the summer, with <u>water only</u> and big brushes.

.5.

Special
Times

Unfortunately, special holiday and family times often mean special dangers and threats to safety. Fire and auto accidents are the most common, as celebrants hurry to their destinations and forget safety rules in the excitement of home celebrations. Liquor can be a serious threat for children if it's left where they can sample it.

Visitors in the home sometimes unwittingly cause problems too. In purses and coat pockets they may bring with them just the kinds of things parents

have so carefully kept out of reach of their children
and they sometimes also bring inappropriate presents
for the kids.

BIRTHDAYS

A birthday party guideline that many parents adopt is
that the number of party guests should be equal to the
age of the birthday child. Obviously this is not always
feasible. However many guests you have, in the
interests of safety, have the parents of 1- and 2-year-
olds stay for the entire party. And serve these parents
only finger foods, if you serve them refreshments at
all, because you don't want to distract them from their
most important function: watching their children! By
age 3, parties work better without other parents
around.

For the safety of both guests and your pet,
banish the dog or cat from the party.

The Indoor Party

If you plan an indoor party for your small child, limit
it to one room only, and childproof that room as
carefully as you possibly can. Leave nothing to
chance; what one bright child doesn't think of, another
will.

♥ Remove from the room any portable electrical appliances and everything breakable or sharp.

♥ Block off any exits to the party room with shut doors or gates. Keep a path open to the bathroom and/or a diaper changing area, but be sure other rooms along the way are not accessible to the children.

♥ If you try a game like "pin the tail on the donkey," be sure to attach tape, not tacks, to tails.

♥ Skip pinatas for a few years. Toddlers and waving, swinging sticks just don't mix. Settle instead for a hunt for soft, safe favors, but be sure everyone "finds" one.

♥ Don't serve small candies, peanuts, popcorn, or even raisins. Children can pick them off the table and choke on them while running around, or even when seated, given the excitement of a party.

♥ If outdoors, be sure you have enough adults to adequately supervise the children. No fewer than one adult per child is suggested if play in any kind of pool is planned.

♥ If your party site is far from home, plan to have parents deliver their own children, unless you have enough car seats for all.

Decorations

Keep your party simple, be it indoors or out. Little
kids won't really appreciate elaborate decorations and
too many decorating materials pose hazards for
children who still put things in their mouths.

♥ Remember that deflated balloons or pieces of
  broken ones are serious suffocation threats.
  Supervise very carefully any handling of balloons
  by small children.

♥ Let balloons make their contribution to the festive
  atmosphere by hanging them high, attached to
  walls, woodwork or chandeliers.

♥ Keep colored crepe paper streamers high, too, so
  children don't put pieces of them in their mouths.

♥ Avoid using a tablecloth, if possible. If you must use
  one, be sure the drop is short enough not to rest on
  children's laps or knees, so they're less apt to pull it
  off.

♥ Be very careful with candles that the birthday child
  will blow out. Long, clean hair catches fire extremely easily. Individual cupcakes with candles to
  blow out for all are fun for older children, but not
  wise for the younger set.

♥ Skip party hats for children who may still be more

interested in chewing or throwing them than in wearing them.

♥ Also avoid blowers, which children usually end up blowing in one anothers' faces.

Favors and Prizes

♥ Avoid small, sharp items as favors as you would avoid them as toys for your own child.

♥ Don't buy "surprise inside" boxes as favors; the surprise may be something you consider definitely dangerous.

♥ Consider as acceptably safe such items as boxes of animal crackers, books (cloth or board for little ones) and small stuffed animals with no detachable parts.

♥ Give balloons as favors only to children old enough not to put pieces in their mouths if they break.

Parties Away from Home

A party at an "away-from-home" spot has the obvious advantages of freeing you of a lot of work and allowing you to come home to a clean house. The bad news is that parties like these are usually overwhelming for children under 5. They're not sophisticated enough yet to be able to handle both a party and the outing's excitement. If you do decide to risk supervising such a crowd, consider a spot that specializes in organizing and producing children's parties. Some are fast-food restaurants, pizza places or ice cream parlors, small, local theme parks or zoos that offer similar inducements, or preschooler gymnastic centers.

♥ Inspect very carefully the premises of any place you're considering, from both atmosphere and safety aspects. Don't take anyone's word that the place is "good." And be aware that a party at one franchised place may differ markedly from one at another, supposedly identical, one.

♥ Be sure the children will be seated for refreshments. It's not safe for any age child to move about while eating, but even more risky for little kids. At home or away, running and eating don't go together.

♥ Ask to see, and inspect carefully, whatever decorations and favors are offered. Favors must not be sharp or breakable, and they must be chewable, unless you're sure all the children are past the stage of putting things in their mouths.

♥ And plan to have with you, just in case, a first aid kit and the phone numbers of any guests' parents who will not be present for the whole party.

HALLOWEEN

Halloween is a favorite holiday for children. The spookiness of it all is wonderful fun, as long as they (and their parents) know they're really safe. Little ones are usually satisfied with simple celebrating—a jack-o-lantern in the window, a wisp of a costume, a trick or treat visit to Grandma or a neighbor or a short stay at a children's party will be enough.

Trick or Treat

Carefree trick or treating has disappeared since Halloween treats that had been laced with poison and inserted with razor blades were discovered. Some parents don't allow trick or treating at all; some inspect minutely every item brought home and throw away more than they keep; others take treat bags to hospitals to be x-rayed. Probably no parent will ever again feel perfectly secure about the practice.

♥ Take your child trick or treating yourself or let him or her go with another adult or an exceptionally reliable teenage sibling or babysitter you can trust with this responsibility.

♥ Let the child visit only the homes of family members or of trusted friends or neighbors.

♥ Don't let your child walk in the street. If there are no sidewalks, have him or her walk right at curbside or across lawns.

♥ Make a firm rule that <u>none</u> of the booty is to be eaten until it has all been inspected at home by a parent. To be sure your child will not be hungry, insist that he or she eat a complete meal before going out.

♥ Go through your child's Halloween treat bag and throw away anything that's not wrapped, unless you know absolutely where and whom it came from. (A piece of fruit from Grandma's, for instance, should pass the test.)

♥ Save any suspicious items and turn them in to police for closer examination.

Costumes

♥ Be sure the fabric in your child's costume is flame resistant.

♥ Make your child clearly visible with generous use of reflector tape.

♥ Keep clothing short and well-fitting enough so the child can walk safely and comfortably.

♥ Check costume accessories carefully for safety. Knives or swords, for example, must be of soft and pliable material.

♥ Paint your child's face with non-toxic makeup instead of putting a mask on him or her. (If you buy cosmetics, avoid any that have ferrocyanide as an ingredient—it's toxic.)

♥ Make your own greasepaint safely and inexpensively: mix 2 teaspoons white shortening with 5 teaspoons cornstarch and 1 teaspoon flour. Add water or a little glycerine to thin, and mix in food coloring. To get a brown color, add an extra teaspoon shortening and 2 teaspoons cocoa before thinning.

Alternatives to Candy Treats

In some neighborhoods, parents have met and decided to avoid candy treats-altogether, both because of poison and razor blade scares and because of the damage sugar can do to teeth. Here are some of the things they've come up with for little kids:

• Inexpensive favors similar to those they give at birthday parties.

• Instant photos they take of the costumed children who come to the door.

• Gift certificates from fast food/ ice cream stores.

• Crayons and small coloring books.

• A bowl full of pennies or nickels that a child grabs a handful of.

Decorations

♥ Don't let a child light a candle in a carved pumpkin or set in one already lit. Make lighting the jack-o-lantern easy and safe for yourself by cutting a hole in the bottom of the pumpkin and setting it over the lit candle.

♥ Better yet, use a flashlight or glow stick and avoid flame altogether.

♥ Consider painting pumpkins instead of carving them for a few years. Even little children can help then.

CHRISTMAS

Christmas is the most exciting time of the year for a 2-or 3-year-old who's at fever pitch and full of the spirit of the season and perhaps the most confusing for a baby or toddler who can't quite grasp the implications of all that's going on. Opportunities for disaster are as great as those for fun and inspiration.

Childproofing the Tree

From the standpoint of safety, should you have a fresh tree, or is an artificial one best? There are points to be made on both sides of the question. The main concern is to make the whatever tree you choose as childproof as possible.

♥ Be sure a fresh tree you buy really <u>is</u> fresh. Test the needles; reject a tree on which they are dry, breaking easily. The freshest tree you can get will be one you cut in the woods yourself, as close as possible to the time you'll put it up.

♥ Saw about two inches off the bottom of the tree to expose fresh tissue that will soak up moisture and, once it's set up, keep the stand filled with water.

♥ Don't position your tree near a heat source.

♥ Consider having a small, tabletop tree for a few years while your child is small. If you do have a large one, set it up in a corner, where it will at least be protected on two sides, and fasten it in some way to woodwork, walls or heavy pieces of furniture. Or try setting it up inside the playpen, as some parents have done.

♥ Take your fresh tree down as soon as the needles begin to fall.

♥ If you buy an artificial tree, avoid one made of metal, which is not safe because of its sharp edges and electrocution potential. <u>Never</u> use electric lights on a metal tree; if they are faulty, they can charge the tree.

♥ Be aware that not all other artificial trees are fire-resistant. Set them up as far from heat sources as you can, as you would a live tree.

Tree Decorations

Your child will be fascinated with the tree and its decorations. You may wish to decorate sparingly for a few years, saving precious and dangerous ornaments until the child is old enough to look without touching.

♥ Test tree lights before you put them on the tree by plugging them in and let them stay lit for a few minutes before putting them on the tree.

♥ Also check any extension cords you plan to use to be sure they aren't frayed. Buy only UL listed cords. And be sure not to overload wattage; add up watts and be sure there are not more than 1500 per outlet.

♥ Don't let light bulbs touch the tree itself—even tiny ones can get hot. Cut needles away, if necessary. On artificial trees, the heat from the lights may deform the needles.

♥ Don't use indoor lights outdoors, their wiring may not withstand severe weather.

♥ Avoid bubbling lights; they contain toxic chemicals

that can escape if they're broken. <u>Never</u> use
candles to light a tree of any kind.

♥ Turn off tree lights when you leave the house,
  always by unplugging them from the wall outlet.

♥ Use only flame-resistant, non-breakable ornaments
  while your child is small, and hang them high,
  where they can't be reached.

♥ Avoid using strings of real popcorn or cranberries
  on the tree for a few years, because your small child
  will reason that if one decoration is edible, all must
  be. For the same reason, don't use ornaments that
  look like food.

♥ Be sure tinsel, if you must use it, is lead-free.

Holiday Plants

♥ Skip the mistletoe and holly decorations while your
  child is small, because the berries of both are
  poisonous if more than a few are swallowed and the
  leaves, if lodged in the larynx, obstruct breathing
  and may cause inflammatory reactions.

♥ Consider dispensing with poinsettias, too, or at
  least place them high. The white, milky juice in
  their stems should not be ingested, and it also
  irritates the skin of some children and adults.

A Cozy Holiday Fire

Few, if any, creature comforts are potentially more dangerous than a cheerful fire in the fireplace. There are a few important "don'ts":

♥ Don't hang the Christmas stockings above a burning fire in the fireplace.

♥ Don't burn wrappings, trees or wreaths in the fireplace. They burst into flame too fast and burn too hot to be safe.

♥ Don't let children throw <u>anything</u> into a fire.

♥ Don't leave a fire unattended, and don't let one burn overnight.

OTHER HOLIDAYS

Each holiday offers a threat or two to safety unless parents use the same caution and common sense they employ every other day of the year.

Easter

♥ Don't let your children eat hard boiled eggs they find in egg hunts you don't plan and supervise yourself, since you don't know how long they have been unrefrigerated.

♥ Refrigerate your own dyed eggs both before and after using them.

Independence Day: 4th of July

It has been said that some 10,000 injuries are suffered every year by people who use fireworks, about 1300 of which are to the eyes. Tragically, 40 percent of those who suffer fireworks-related eye injuries that cause permanent eye damage, visual disability or actual loss of an eye are children.

♥ <u>Allow absolutely no small fireworks, even sparklers, for children under school age.</u> It's best not to buy them at all, even if your state is one that allows their sale.

♥ Plan to enjoy nighttime fireworks displays put on by clubs or community organizations.

♥ Let children make noise safely by popping blown-up paper bags. Or show them how to pop the bubbles in plastic bubble wrap by squeezing them between fingers, stomping on them or riding over them on trikes.

.6.

Childproofing Your Child

You've childproofed indoors and outdoors as thoroughly as you can, you've considered every possibility for trouble both at home and away, and you're super careful when you celebrate special occasions. Still, concerns that center around daily living—feeding, clothing, entertaining and educating your child—often arise.

AT MEALTIME

Cleanliness in handling and serving food is very important in the prevention of food poisoning and the spread of infections. Hands should be washed before starting to prepare a meal and after handling raw meat, especially chicken. All the kitchen areas where food is dealt with should be kept scrupulously clean. Your child will learn from observing these sanitary precautions just as he or she learns and imitates you as you practice other good hygiene habits.

Infant Formula

♥ Prepare your baby's formula according to the directions on the container or those your doctor gives you. Be sure all the tools and equipment you use are clean.

♥ Don't store formula at high temperatures or it may curdle. Dispose of or return to the market any formula you suspect has curdled; it may cause mild stomach upset, diarrhea or even vomiting.

♥ Likewise, don't use formula in damaged containers.

♥ Check expiration dates on formula. Don't buy or use any on which the date has passed.

Baby Food

♥ Avoid honey or corn syrup for a baby under a year old. There's danger of infant botulism, and since both are nutritionally non-essential, it's not worth taking a chance.

♥ Keep baby dry cereals away from heat and moisture so they don't become infested with weevils or other insects.

♥ Before opening a jar of baby food, check to be sure that the small circle on the lid is depressed and the seal is not broken. Listen for a "pop" sound as the vacuum seal breaks when you open the jar.

♥ Refrigerate opened baby food and use it within two or three days.

♥ Don't feed a child out of a baby food jar or store leftovers from the baby's dishes in the jar. Saliva from the baby's spoon contains enzymes that break down starches.

♥ Don't heat food in the container if only part of it will be eaten and the remainder stored. Reheating can spoil taste and texture and, worse, can lower nutritional value.

♥ Prepare your own baby food if you wish, according to instructions you'll find in many parenting books and articles. Or look for frozen baby food in some areas. Do be careful not to overcook vegetables and lose nutrients.

Choking

Choking occurs when something in a child's mouth gets into the trachea (air passage) instead of the esophagus (food passage). The trachea becomes blocked, and air cannot get into the child's lungs. Infants are apt to choke if they are given solid foods too early, before they are able to coordinate chewing and swallowing. Toddlers are vulnerable because they often do not chew their food enough, or at all. The best insurance against choking is knowing how to relieve it. Become familiar with the correct measures to deal with choking as they are described in your first aid book—back blows/chest pressures for a baby, the Heimlich maneuver for an older child—so that you'll be prepared if you ever need to use one of them. (The American Heart Association includes instruction in the Heimlich maneuver in its approved CPR course.)

MOST COMMON FOODS THAT CAUSE CHOKING

Hot dogs	Nuts
Chunks of meat	Popcorn
Grapes	Raisins
Hard candy	Raw carrots
Chunky peanut butter	Ice Cubes

♥ Don't ever leave a baby or small child alone while he or she is eating.

♥ Insist that your child eat in an upright position. This rule applies to babies, too, so a bottle should not be propped for an infant who's lying down.

♥ Stress the importance of taking small bites and chewing food well. Cut hot dogs and carrots length-wise or into small, narrow pieces. Peel and/or half grapes. Round and slippery foods are the most common hazards.

♥ Supervise your child's eating extra carefully if you have applied a teething anesthetic to his or her gums within the past hour or so. The products sometimes impair a child's ability to swallow.

♥ DO NOT INTERFERE WITH A CHOKING CHILD WHO IS BREATHING, COUGHING OR SPEAK-ING. Natural reflexes usually do the trick . Re-move anything visible to the eye (versus poking your finger in the mouth—and possibly the item down the trachea).

♥ If your child chokes and cannot breathe, call for help immediately, then administer appropriate treatment. If possible, let someone else do the calling. Don't wait for help to arrive and don't try to get to an emergency department, there's rarely time. Irreversible brain damage can result from the lack of oxygen to the brain.

♥ Have your child examined by a doctor after a choking incident, even if you think recovery is complete. There may still be fragments in the upper respiratory tract.

CLOTHING

We tend to think more about whether clothing is appropriate, attractive and economical than we do about whether it is safe for our children. There are certain things to consider, though.

Sleepwear

CPSC requires that all children's sleepwear to size 14, and all fabric from which sleepwear may be sewn at home, be made of flame resistant fabric. However, such requirements do not apply to other garments that may be worn for sleeping such as diapers.

♥ Be aware that hand-me-down or garage sale infants' and children's sleepwear may not be flame resistant or may have been laundered improperly so that flame-retardant properties are damaged. Some older garments may also contain the flame-retardant TRIS, which several years ago was discovered to be cancer-causing and made illegal.

♥ Read the labels on sleepwear and follow laundering instructions. The effectiveness of flame-retardants used in some fabrics is reduced by buildup caused by soap (as opposed to laundry detergent).

Daywear

♥ Be sure that decals or parts of them, such as button eyes on animal cutouts, are firmly attached on such items as sweatshirts and bibs, so your child cannot pry them off and put them in his or her mouth.

♥ Check buttons on small children's clothing frequently to be sure they can't be pulled off and swallowed or choked upon. Choose clothes that fasten with zippers, snaps or Velcro when you can.

♥ Cut off any unnecessary long strings on children's clothing and hats so they can't catch on playground equipment or furniture. Also trim loose threads on a baby's clothing so they won't catch tiny fingers, toes or nails.

♥ Never use pins to hold children's clothing together, even for a short time.

♥ Teach a child learning to put on clothes to pull a zipper up and away from clothes to keep it from catching on skin and cutting or bruising.

♥ Dispose immediately of any thin plastic bags in which your children's clothing is returned from dry cleaners.

♥ Don't let your child wear clothing with his or her name on it, especially if you pick him or her up from a nursery school. Abductors sometimes make use of a child's name, pretending to be family friends charged with picking up the child.

Safety Measures ON Your Child

♥ To help keep your baby from slipping on hardwood floors, draw several stripes on socks or pajama feet with the plastic "pen" used for painting T-shirts. The paint dries to form a raised plastic design.

♥ Rough up the soles of slippery new shoes or apply tub appliques or a strip or two of masking tape.

♥ Put socks or bootees on a crawling baby's hands, which will let him or her be mobile but will discourage picking up small undesirables.

♥ Wipe your child's shoestrings with a wet cloth before you tie them. They'll shrink as they dry and should stay tied all day, preventing many trips and falls. Or limit yourself to Velcro closing shoes and avoid the danger of untied shoes altogether.

TEACHING CHILDREN ABOUT DANGERS

Talk to your child about safety as you go about your daily activities, just as you talk about other things you want him or her to absorb. Kids learn a great deal this way, "by osmosis," as it were. Another way your child will develop good safety habits is by observing and copying you—so be sure your example is a good one! Sometimes a great deal in the way of maturity is expected of children, especially if they are physically or mentally developed beyond other children their age. It's important to remember that youngsters are not small adults, and that they are not qualified by experience or by nature to make decisions upon which their lives may depend.

Everyday

♥ Consistently use words that your child will come to associate with safety, words like <u>danger</u>, <u>poison</u>, <u>hot</u>, <u>sharp</u>. And words that mean you must be obeyed immediately: *No!.. Don't touch!...Stop!*

♥ Make reasonable but inflexible safety rules, and repeat them often. Remember that the parent/child relationship is not always a democratic one. Don't make a game of safety issues; be firm.

♥ Help your child learn to anticipate the consequences of foolish risk-taking. Ask questions when you're reading to him or her or watching television together: "Why shouldn't a child do that?" "What might happen if that boy rides his bike into the street?"

♥ Praise your child for showing good safety behavior and actions that show he or she is thinking ahead.

♥ Look for library books that stress safety. The "Safety Town Series" by Dorothy Chlad is one set suitable for young children. It includes books in both English and Spanish on safe behavior in many everyday situations. Some involve water, automobile riding, playgrounds, poisons, crossing the street and fire.

In Specific Situations

Your approach to specific safety concerns will be based both on where you live and on what "kind" of a child yours is. City life is different from life in a small town or in the country, apartment living calls for different safety skills than living in a house. If you're dealing with a natural risk-taker who's always anxious to try everything and never worried about being hurt, your safety talks and examples will be on the strong side. If you have a careful child who goes into new situations cautiously, anticipating trouble, you may need only to mention a danger in passing.

♥ Explain, as you're working in the kitchen, why you are careful with hot pans and sharp knives and why you protect your child from coming into contact with them.

♥ Plant the seeds about street safety as you walk about your neighborhood. Explain why we cross only at crosswalks, obey the signals and watch and listen for traffic.

♥ Have your child repeatedly practice reciting his or her name, address and phone number as early as possible.

♥ Have a family fire discussion. Where will you all meet OUTSIDE the house if a fire occurs? Teach the concept of *Stop, Drop and Roll*, to put out flames on clothes to an older child.

♥ Begin casual discussions about strangers when your child is about 3, especially if you live in a large city. Talk about who is a stranger and who is not, about how children should not take anything from strangers or obey commands from them to "come here" or "get in the car."

PETS

Pets can be wonderful for kids, providing companion-
ship and great learning experiences. Dogs and cats
are most common, but others—birds, fish, rabbits,
gerbils and other rodents—are popular too. The
advantage of having a dog or cat is that, with a little
luck, it can be a companion and playmate to your
child for many years. Other kinds of pets should be
kept out of reach of young children, since they can
inflict hurts or be hurt themselves. Not advised for
families with children are exotic or wild pets of any
kind, such as baby foxes, wolf cubs or monkeys. Hold
off on acquiring a pet for a young child who is showing
signs of asthma or allergies—pet hair often exacer-
bates these conditions.

Making the Proper Introductions

If you have the child before you get the pet, do a little
research, to be sure you get the animal that best suits
your family. Topping your list of requirements, if
you're considering a dog or cat, should be gentleness
and patience. For example. hounds, retrievers and
spaniels are often good with children, while chows,
terriers and German shepherds don't have that
reputation (though obviously there are many excep-
tions).

Whichever has come first—the pet or the baby—may need a little help in adjusting to the presence of the other.

♥ Bring home a blanket or diaper you've put into your baby's hospital bassinet and let the dog or cat that's already part of your family get used to the baby's scent before homecoming day.

♥ Watch the initial reactions of a pet and your child carefully; supervise their interchanges closely for awhile.

♥ Pay extra attention to your pet, if you're introducing a new baby into your household, or if the pet is a stray whose background you don't know about.

♥ Help your child learn to pat your dog or cat softly in the appropriate places and to play gently.

♥ Remember that puppies like to chew, just as babies do, and that their teeth are very sharp. Without intending to, your new pet can hurt your baby.

Health and Hygiene

Pests such as fleas and even some illnesses can be transferred from pets to human beings, so you'll want to establish good hygiene habits. Keep your pet clean, take a young one for routine checkups with the veterinarian and keep its immunizations up to date.

♥ Have your veterinarian check a new pet to be sure it's free of fleas, lice, ticks and worms and does not have throat or skin infections.

♥ Control fleas and/or lice on your pet, but be careful not to use the special powders and baths that contain harmful pesticides in the same room with your child. Don't put a flea collar on a dog or cat that a child will be handling; pesticides it contains are also harmful.

♥ Keep the cat litter box clean and out of your child's reach (put it in a bathtub, a closet with a safety latch on the outside so it can be kept partially open, or in a corner where you can put a safety gate across the corner.)

♥ Clean up dog feces in an outdoor area in which your child will play.

♥ Don't allow your pet to sleep with your child. If it shows a desire to get into the crib with a baby, put a gate at the nursery door.

♥ Teach your child to wash his or her hands after playing with a pet.

♥ 7 ♥

Poison Prevention

Babies and small children are interested in everything around them—it's their business to explore and experiment and learn. Unfortunately, this curiosity leads many of them to taste and chew and feel poisonous substances every year and become very ill or even die. It's the responsibility of parents and caretakers to keep all poisonous substances out of sight, out of reach, and out of bounds for children.

CHILDREN ACT FAST...AND SO DO POISONS!

Almost half of all poisonings are from medicines and vitamins. And detergents are ingested more than any other household product.

Your regional Poison Center is listed on the inside cover of your phone book, under "Emergency" in the yellow pages or under "Poison" in the white (or business) pages. Most areas are covered by a regional Poison Center. Be sure to know yours! And then contact them for telephone stickers with their phone number on them. If there is not a certified center in your area, your nearest poison control center may be located in a hospital emergency room.

Read the labels on all chemical and cosmetic products you buy. There are products which are less hazardous than others. Let their "signal" words be your guide:

POISON means highly toxic
DANGER means highly toxic, corrosive and/or
   flammable
WARNING means moderately toxic
CAUTION means slightly toxic

♥ Be sure to leave products in their original containers that clearly identify the contents. Be sure to read ALL label instructions before using a product, and store household chemicals away from foods.

♥ Buy unscented products so children are less prone to eat or drink them.

Buy a bottle of syrup of ipecac to have in your pantry should it ever be needed. It induces vomiting within 20 minutes. A one ounce bottle costs less than $2. Every bottle is stamped with an expiration date. When it expires, replace it. Get a second bottle to keep in your handbag or in the car's glove compartment. After all lots of poisonings occur away from home.

SHOULD A POISONING ACTUALLY OCCUR

Be aware that the two basic types of poisons—CAUSTIC (meaning they cause burning) and NON CAUSTIC—require very different types of treatment. Complete lists of each would require space not available here, but a few examples can be given. The caustic category includes such products as drain opener, toilet bowl cleaner, laundry detergent, electric dishwasher detergent, oven cleaner, rust remover, battery acid and some health and beauty products such as permanent wave solution. Among noncaustics toxins are most health and beauty aids, some (not all) petroleum products such as gasoline, kerosene, and furniture polish, some plants, medicines and cigarettes.

♥ If poison has been taken by mouth, remove any you can get at. Then call your Poison Center <u>immediately</u>. Chances are good that with instruction, you will be able to treat your child at home.

♥ If your child is unconscious, has throat soreness, excessive drowsiness or seems very ill, call your emergency medical service at 911 and/or head for the hospital's emergency room.

♥ If for some reason you can't reach help at the moment, give the child a glass of milk or water, if he or she is conscious and willing to drink it. Do not force any liquids.

♥ NEVER GIVE SYRUP OF IPECAC WITHOUT FIRST CALLING YOUR POISON CENTER AND BEING ADVISED TO DO SO. Never give syrup of ipecac or otherwise induce vomiting if you know or even suspect that the poison ingested was in the caustic category.

♥ Save the container. Bring it with you to the phone. You may need to describe it over the phone, or your doctor may want to see it if you are advised to go to a hospital.

♥ If poison has affected the child's skin, remove any contaminated clothing and flood the skin with water for 15-20 minutes, then wash gently with soap and water. Then call your Poison Center.

♥ If poison is in the child's eyes, hold eyelids open and pour cool water into the eyes for 15-20 minutes. Then call the Poison Center. Don't let the child rub the eyes and don't hold a child's head under running water from a faucet, either.

PHILODENDRUM   POTHOS   DIFFENBACHIA   MISTLETOE

Indoor Poisonous Plants

Bird of Paradise pods   Jerusalem Cherry
Caladium   Mistletoe
Christmas Pepper   Philodendron
Diefenbachia (Dumb Cane)   Pothos
English Ivy

Non-Poisonous Indoors

African Violet   Kalanchoe
Asparagus Fern   Palm (all types)
Begonia   Peperomia
Boston Fern   Poinsettia (but can cause
Christmas Cactus   irritation)
Dracaena   Purple Passion Vine
Easter Lily   Sansevieria (Snake Plant)
Flame Violet   Schefflera
Fuchsia   Spider Plant
Gloxinia   Tahitian Bridal Veil
Jade Plant   Ti Plant

HYDRANGEA   DAFFODIL   AZALEA   POISON IVY

Outdoor Poisonous Plants

Azalea
Bloodroot
Caladium
Castor Bean
Daffodil and Jonquil
Delphinium
English Ivy
Fruit pits from any tree fruits
Foxglove
Holly Berries
Hyacinth
Hydrangea
Iris
Jack in the Pulpit
Lantana
Larkspur
Laurel

Lily of the Valley
Morning Glory
Mushrooms (most)
Narcissus (bulbs)
Nicotiana
Oleander
Pokeweed
Poison Ivy
Privet
Rhododendron
Rhubarb (leaves)
Sweet Pea
Tobacco
Tulip
Wisteria
Yew

Non-Poisonous Outdoor

Bachelor Button
Coleus
Dandelion
Impatiens
Marigold

Petunia
Rose
Salvia
Viburnum

POISONOUS HOUSEHOLD PRODUCTS

After-shave lotion
Alcoholic beverages
Ammonia
Anti-freeze
Aspirin
 and acetaminophen
Auto Wax
Baby Powder
Bleach
Boric Acid
Charcoal-Lighting Fluid
Cleaning Fluid
Correction Fluid
Cosmetics
Dishwasher Detergent
Drain Cleaner
Fertilizer
Furniture Polish
Gasoline
Hair Spray
Insecticides
 and pest strips
Insect Repellent
Iodine

Lamp oil
Laundry Products
Laxatives
Lighter Fluid
Lye
Mercury Batteries
Motor Oil
Mothballs
Mouthwash
Nail Polish
Nail Polish Remover
Oven Cleaner
Paint
Paint Thinner
Perfume
Room Deodorizer
Rubbing Alcohol
Solvents
Tobacco
Toilet Bowl Cleaner
Turpentine
Vitamins
Weed Killer
Windshield Washer
 Solution

There are, despite the length of the previous lists,
many common <u>non-poisonous</u> household products.
But since quantity can make the difference if something is toxic (some things not listed as toxic can
become so depending on quantity ingested or reformu-
lation of a product, etc), it is not fair to even try to list
such items here. Don't hesitate to call your Poison
Control center when you have a question. Better to
be safe than sorry.

A list of certified regional poison centers may
be obtained from: American Association of Poison
Control Centers, 3800 Reservoir Road NW,   Washington, DC 20007.

INDEX

More books by Vicki Lansky:

- FEED ME I'M YOURS (Cookbook)
- TAMING OF THE CANDY MONSTER (Cookbook)
- KIDS COOKING (Cookbook)
- MICROWAVE COOKING FOR KIDS (Cookbook)
- PRACTICAL PARENTING™ TIPS, Ages 1-5
- BABYPROOFING BASICS
- TOILET TRAINING
- KOKO BEAR'S NEW POTTY
- WELCOMING YOUR SECOND BABY
- A NEW BABY AT KOKO BEAR'S HOUSE
- DEAR BABYSITTER HANDBOOK
- GAMES BABIES PLAY
- KOKO BEAR'S BIG EARACHE
  (Preparing Your Child for Ear Tube Surgery)
- GETTING YOUR CHILD TO SLEEP...& BACK TO SLEEP
- GETTING YOUR BABY TO SLEEP (Audiocassette)
- BIRTHDAY PARTIES: Best Tips & Ideas for Ages 1-8
- TROUBLE-FREE TRAVEL WITH CHILDREN
- SING ALONG BIRTHDAY SONGS (Audiocassette)
- SING ALONG TRAVEL SONGS (Audiocassette)
- 101 WAYS TO TELL YOUR CHILD "I LOVE YOU"
- 101 WAYS TO MAKE YOUR CHILD FEEL SPECIAL
- 101 WAYS TO BE A SPECIAL MOM
- 101 WAYS TO BE A SPECIAL DAD
- 101 WAYS TO SAY "I LOVE YOU" (for grown-ups)
- 101 WAYS TO SPOIL YOUR GRANDCHILD
- *Vicki Lansky's* DIVORCE BOOK FOR PARENTS:
  Helping Kids Cope With Divorce and Its Aftermath
- ANOTHER USE FOR...101 Common Household Items
  (as featured in her *Family Circle HELP!* column)
- BAKING SODA, Over 500 Fabulous, Fun and FrugAl Uses

**For a free catalog of all Vicki's books
or to order books (MC, Visa, AmEx)
call 1-800-255-3379 or write
Practical Parenting Books-By-Mail
15245 Minnetonka Blvd., Minnetonka, MN 55345**